What Kids Are Say
Chicken Soup for the (

"I like this book because it shows kids how to forgive, tell the truth, and be good to others. I think it's amazing."

Isaac High, 8

"I really liked *Chicken Soup for the Child's Soul* because lots of emotions ran through me while reading it. It teaches you how to cope with the hard times."

Rachel Brown, 10

"Two thumbs way up!"

Dawson Hughes, 8

"The stories in *Chicken Soup for the Child's Soul* were so great that I could read them every day. I'll read them to my kids when I get to be a mom."

Sierra Hynes, 8

"I think people should read *Chicken Soup for the Child's Soul* because the stories are about caring, accepting others, and being nice."

John Hughes, 10

"I think every kid should read this book because it helps you learn things about growing up."

Christian Nunez, 11

"I especially liked the animal stories."

Alexis Bounopane, 9

"The stories in *Chicken Soup for the Child's Soul* were very good, and they made me think about my life."

Belma Omanouic, 10

"I liked the stories in *Chicken Soup for the Child's Soul* because I could picture them in my head. It was such a fun book to read."

Robyn Bajraktari, 9

"*Chicken Soup for the Child's Soul* really helps out in tight situations like with a friend or family member. I think people of all ages should read it."

Isabelle Evans, 10

"*Chicken Soup for the Child's Soul* is a great way for kids to learn that there are some people just like them in this world."

Zoë Hall, 10

CHICKEN SOUP FOR THE CHILD'S SOUL

Chicken Soup for the Child's Soul
Character-Building Stories to Read with Kids Ages 5-8
Jack Canfield, Mark Victor Hansen, Patty Hansen, Irene Dunlap

Published by Backlist, LLC,
a unit of Chicken Soup for the Soul Publishing, LLC. www.chickensoup.com

Front cover design by Andrea Perrine Brower
Originally published in 2007 by Health Communications, Inc.

Back cover and spine redesign by Pneuma Books, LLC

Distributed to the booktrade by Simon & Schuster. SAN: 200-2442

Publisher's Cataloging-in-Publication Data
(Prepared by The Donohue Group)

Chicken soup for the child's soul : character-building stories to read with
    kids ages 5-8 / [compiled by] Jack Canfield ... [et al.].

    p. : ill. ; cm.

    Originally published: Deerfield Beach, FL : Health Communications, c2007.
    Interest age level: 005-008.
    ISBN: 978-1-62361-115-6

    1. Children--Conduct of life--Juvenile literature. 2. Children--Conduct of
life--Anecdotes. 3. Children--Conduct of life. 4. Anecdotes. I. Canfield, Jack,
1944-

BJ1631 .C455 2012
170/.44   2012945887

PRINTED IN THE UNITED STATES OF AMERICA
on acid free paper

22 21 20   07 08 09 10 11

CHICKEN SOUP FOR THE CHILD'S SOUL

Character-Building Stories to Read with Kids Ages 5–8

Jack Canfield
Mark Victor Hansen
Patty Hansen
Irene Dunlap

Backlist, LLC, a unit of
Chicken Soup for the Soul Publishing, LLC
Cos Cob, CT
www.chickensoup.com

Contents

8. LOOKING ON THE BRIGHT SIDE

Introduction

Good character and integrity are contributing factors to a successful and fulfilling life—something we all want for our kids. Yet children today live in a world where they are often confused by what they hear in the news and by how they see people treat each other.

While most of us strive to develop positive character traits in our kids, we find there are few true role models left for our children to look up to. And we recognize that good character is not always inherently given to us, but is taught by example and through individual choices we make each day.

John Luther regarded it this way: "Good character is more to be praised than outstanding talent. Most talents are to some extent a gift. Good character, by contrast, is not given to us. We have to build it piece by piece—by thought, choice, courage, and determination."

Since *Chicken Soup for the Kid's Soul* was released in 1998, we have found a resounding theme in the constant stream of letters we receive from the kids who read our books. They have assured us that the true stories of universal experiences and life lessons from kids (and adults who haven't forgotten what it's like to be a kid) give them perspective, shape the way they approach life situations, and give them hope for their futures.

The book you're holding is part of our ongoing response to those letters, and the continuous need to assist kids in building their own good moral base and strength of character that will serve them throughout their lives. Chosen specifically for children five to eight years old, these stories offer young readers a chance to discover how children just like themselves react and behave when confronted with difficult situations that test their character.

Through each chapter, without moralizing or preaching, stories about how kids have learned to adjust to and even accept tough changes, find forgiveness, take responsibility, or share with those in need will inspire readers and help them understand that life is a journey, made up of the decisions and lessons we learn from each and every day. It is our hope that because of the actions and strength of character exemplified by kids in these stories, the children in your realm of influence will discover a pathway for making good life decisions and, in turn, help make the world a better place.

So we encourage you to take a few minutes each day to sit down and read these stories with children or have them read these stories to you. The time spent reading together will be undoubtedly special and priceless, while each positive lesson they learn from this book will last their lifetimes.

1

THINKING OF OTHERS

I was miserable at school on the first day.
No kind words had come my way.
It seemed that everyone was in groups or pairs.
I was the only one sitting among empty chairs.
But what happened next changed my point of view.
I heard a voice saying, "Hi, can I sit with you?"
Joy went through me as I saw kindness in her eyes.
The impact of that single word came as a surprise.
Now I have tons of friends 'cause of something I do.
I greet everyone with "Hi," and maybe you should too.

Jessica Bolandina, 13

My Lady

"Grrrrrrr."

The soft growl made me stop in my tracks as I was walking across my neighbor's backyard. Was it a bear? Maybe a wolverine had gotten into the yard in search of food.

My eyes came to rest on the shadows under the small fishing boat that was up on blocks. As they became adjusted to the dark, I realized that the growl was coming from a large dog.

"It's okay," I said. "I'm just passing through."

The dog stared at me, its short black coat dull and matted, then it groaned and laid its large head on its paws. I paused for a moment, taking in how skinny it was, and then realized that my neighbors didn't have a dog. I knew what I needed to do. I whispered to the dog, "I'll be right back . . . don't go anywhere."

I ran to my house, my heart pounding as I raced through the door, grabbed a paper bag, and filled it with some food. I raced back out into the early spring evening. The air made my breath fog as I panted, and the chill froze my fingers as I clutched the little bag of food.

When I got to the boat, I slowed down. The dog was too tired and hungry to even lift its head. I came closer carefully and noticed that it was a girl. I placed the food on the grass in front of her and moved back, ready to bolt if she was mean.

"It's okay, girl. I brought you some food," I said.

She lifted up her large head and cocked it to the side as though she was deciding whether to believe me or not. Then, with a loud groan, she stood up and walked to the food. It disappeared in no time. When she finished, she sat down and stared at me. I knew without a doubt that she wanted more.

"I can get you more, but you need to stay right here," I explained as I started to back up. "Stay here, okay?"

I ran back through the yard to my house, my thoughts on nothing except the dog. When I stepped through the doors, I realized that I was late getting home. My dad was waiting for me.

"Where have you been, Sirena?" he asked.

My breath came out in gasps as I explained, "There is a sick dog in the neighbor's yard, and I was giving her some food."

My dad looked at me, sighed, and then started out the door with me following close behind. To our surprise, we found the skinny dog sitting in our driveway, ears forward, waiting for me. My dad went to reach for her only to have her skitter away. She looked at him, eyes big with fear, and then she looked at me and ran behind me to hide. Laughing, my dad said, "Looks like you have a patient."

I was overjoyed and got busy taking care of her. I set up a bed for her in the laundry room and put out some food and water. As I comforted her, I realized that we had already become friends. I couldn't bear to send her off to the dog shelter, so I walked into the kitchen to plead my case. I explained to my parents how I would walk her and care for her. I told them that I wasn't too young to have a pet, and I could prove it to them. In the end, it was decided that I could care for her while we looked for her owner.

As the days went by, no one came to claim her, and finally my parents let me keep her. I named her Lady, and she quickly became my best friend.

Months later, as I was walking down the road with Lady, a dark car pulled up alongside us. Lady glanced over, and then started jumping and barking. A large smile spread across her face. I knew before the car door even opened that Lady had found her original owner.

He was tall and thin, with large brown hands that hugged and patted Lady. She wriggled in his arms, licking his long face, and I could see the happiness in his brown eyes as he looked up at me. "I've been looking for Rocky," he said to me. "It looks like you have been taking good care of her."

So Lady's real name was Rocky. I blinked the tears from my eyes as I looked at him. "Is she your dog?" I asked, already knowing the answer.

"Yes, she is. She ran away a few months ago, and I couldn't find her. I'm glad she found someone to take care of her."

My hands loosened on the leash as I looked at her. She was so happy and excited, dancing in circles, tongue hanging out the side of her mouth as she looked between us. My words came in bursts. "So . . . I guess . . . you want her . . . back, huh? She's yours . . . and she's a really good dog. She should go with you."

The man looked at my outstretched hand for a few minutes, his brown eyes thoughtful. Then he stood up, smiled, and said, "It looks like she's happy right where she is. I wouldn't feel right taking her from someone she needs. So I think you should keep her, if you still want her."

A smile lit up my face as I nodded, too happy to say anything. I watched him climb back into his car and slowly drive away, waving to us as he did. My steps were light as I continued walking, Lady in step beside me, right where she belonged.

Sirena Van Schaik

The Right Thing to Do

Although I was trying to concentrate on cursive writing and the fours times tables at school, I couldn't stop thinking about my beautiful Halloween costume waiting for me at home. I was going to be an angel with wings! My mother had made the wings out of cardboard and leftover Christmas tinsel, and I thought she had made magic.

It was certainly better than last year's costume when I had been a female Frankenstein. That costume was a hand-me-down from my brother Kevin. We were only about a year apart in age, and we had to share everything—including germs.

The morning of Halloween, I was surprised to find that I could hardly swallow. As my brother hung his head down from the top bunk, he did not have to say a word. I knew that he was sick, too. I couldn't think of anything more terrible, especially on Halloween.

It turned out to be a rainy Halloween night. As the rain fell, so did my tears whenever I looked at my beautiful costume. My mother tried to make the best of it by telling us how much fun it would be to stay home and give out candy. I admit it was exciting to see what television character or creature our neighborhood friends would be, but it still was not quite as thrilling as going trick-or-treating.

When it was time for bed, just as Kevin and I were climbing into our bunkbeds, we heard a knock on the front door. Before long, our mother came to our bedroom and told us we needed to come out.

On the front porch stood the four Montgomery children. Before we could say a word, they handed my brother and me each a pillowcase full of candy! My mother told them to thank their mom for her thoughtful idea, but Bonnie, one of the older kids, replied, "Mom didn't tell us to do this—we just wanted to."

Still surprised, we thanked the Montgomery children and watched them walk away. That's when we noticed that they only had two pillowcases, even though there were four of them. They had actually given away their own pillowcases full of candy. I couldn't believe that anybody would do that, especially when their mother hadn't even made them!

As we poured the bags of candy out on the bedroom floor, we were in for another surprise. Mom told us that we did not have to go back to bed and that we could actually stay up and sort our candy. I think my mother had also missed going trick-or-treating as much we had, and so we offered some of the candy to her. After a few trades with my brother, my mother said firmly that it was time for lights out.

Saying my good-night prayers, I remembered a special word of thanks for the Montgomery children and their gifts of the pillowcases full of candy. I even finally forgave Jimmy Montgomery for destroying my cardboard doll bed the time he had tried to crawl into it.

That seemed like the right thing to do to trade for the pillowcases full of candy generously given to a couple of sick neighborhood friends.

Stephanie Ray Brown

Friends of the Heart

*Kind words and good deeds are eternal.
You never know where their influence will
end.*

H. Jackson Brown, Jr.

Ariana caught another whiff and tried to hold her breath. She moved away slightly, but Ashley only moved closer and continued talking.

Ariana thought to herself, *Why does she always have to sit next to me?* She inched away some more until she touched elbows with the girl next to her. Ashley didn't seem to notice that Ariana was trying to move away, and she leaned in closer. Ariana felt trapped. She wanted badly to tell Ashley that she didn't smell very good. But how could she without hurting her feelings? Instead, she gathered the remains of her lunch to throw in the trash, thankful for the excuse to get some fresh air.

She looked back to see Ashley eating quietly. Ashley's hair was stringy and tangled, like it needed a good washing, and her clothes were wrinkled and stained. All the other kids talked and laughed with each other. No one talked and laughed with Ashley.

Ariana forced herself to go back to the table and take her seat. She was stuck with Ashley today, but vowed that she would not get stuck with her tomorrow.

When Ariana got home from school, she complained to her mother. "There's this girl named Ashley who likes to sit next to me in school, but she smells bad."

"She's probably having a tough day," said her mother.

"No, it's not just one day. She smells bad a lot," Ariana explained. "Nobody else likes to sit next to her, either."

"Well, try to be nice to her," said her mother. "Maybe she's having a hard time at home. You never know what a person's home life is like."

For the rest of the week, Ariana tried to be a good friend to Ashley. There were times when they had fun talking and playing together, especially on the days that Ashley bathed. But the days when she smelled bad, which was most of the time, Ariana still found it very hard to be her friend.

One morning, while getting her hair combed for school, Ariana brought the subject up again with her mother.

"I don't want to be friends with Ashley anymore," she told her.

"Why? Is she mean to you?" asked her mother, twisting Ariana's hair into a ponytail.

"No. She stinks!" Ariana scrunched up her nose. "And her clothes are dirty. She wore the same shirt two days in a row. That's disgusting."

Her mother's hands froze in midair. Ariana turned to see what the matter was. Her mother looked upset. Ariana wondered what she had said to make her mother react this way.

"I don't think you understand Ashley's situation, so let me ask you this. . . ." Her mother's tone was serious. "Who makes sure that your hair is combed every morning so you'll look nice when you go to school?"

"You do," answered Ariana.

"Who makes sure you're bathed and cleaned every day? And your clothes are washed and neatly ironed?"

"You and Daddy," Ariana said again.

"Do you live in a nice home? Do you have enough to eat?"

Ariana nodded, beginning to feel guilty. She was starting to understand now. Ashley couldn't help her situation because she was only seven years old—the same age as Ariana. Grown-ups are supposed to take care of kids.

"Why doesn't her family take better care of her?" Ariana asked.

"Not all children live in the best situation," her

mother said. "The best thing you can do for Ashley is to treat her with kindness and compassion."

Ariana bit her bottom lip. Sadness for Ashley filled her heart. She vowed that from now on she would be the best friend that she could be to Ashley.

At school, Ariana kept her vow. She let Ashley sit next to her. Other times, she voluntarily sat next to Ashley. She partnered with Ashley to help with her schoolwork. On the days that Ashley smelled bad, she moved away a little or politely asked Ashley for a little room. She was always careful not to hurt Ashley's feelings.

As the months passed, Ariana discovered that she enjoyed talking and hanging out with Ashley. She no longer saw her as the girl who smelled bad, but as a friend with a kind and warm heart.

At the end of the school year, the second grade prepared to go on a field trip to the zoo. The day before the field trip, the teacher announced that the class needed to bring in a lunch from home. Ashley was absent, and Ariana worried that her friend would not have a lunch because Ashley always ate the school lunches.

Ariana couldn't call Ashley because she didn't know her telephone number. So, the next day, Ariana asked her mom to make an extra lunch and some snacks for Ashley—just in case.

"You have a good spirit, Ariana," said her mother. "I'm very proud of you!"

When Ariana got to school, she discovered that she

had been right. Ashley had not brought a lunch for the field trip.

When Ariana gave the lunch to Ashley, she saw tears well up in Ashley's eyes. Ariana was surprised at Ashley's reaction because after all, she was only doing what true friends do for each other. Ashley was her friend—and they were friends of the heart.

Ariana Morgan Bridges as told to Robin Smith Bridges

The Key to Bethany's Heart

The unselfish effort to bring cheer to others will be the beginning of a happier life for ourselves.

Helen Keller

"Come on in! The water's great," I assured Bethany. I wanted to reach out to my new foster sister, to let her know that she could trust us. We'd never let her down the way her mother had done.

Bethany shook her head, not budging from her seat on the shore. She scowled at the waves that rushed in from the sea. She seemed angry to be here with a strange family and a girl who was trying too hard to be her sister. She hadn't asked for her mother to suddenly walk out of her life, leaving her in foster care. And she hadn't asked to join my family on vacation.

My parents walked up to Bethany. She stiffened when

Mom knelt and put her arm around her shoulders.

"I know it's hard for you, Bethany. Please try to understand that we only want to love and help you."

Tears filled Bethany's eyes. She didn't want our help. She wanted to go back to her own life. Yet, part of her knew that it wasn't our fault that she had to be with us. She nodded and murmured "I know," but I could tell she was hurting inside.

Bethany sat with her head down as Mom and Dad walked away. She picked up a small clamshell that had washed onto the shore and rubbed the smooth surface with her fingers. Once, a living creature had claimed it as home, but now it was as cold and empty as Bethany's heart.

I stood up and watched a small wave come crashing in.

"What good does it do to sit here and miss all the fun?" I asked Bethany.

"I don't exactly feel like having *fun*. My life isn't perfect like yours, Sarah."

"I've always thought that my life would be perfect if I only had a sister. I just want to be your best friend."

When Bethany didn't reply, I felt like walking away and having my own fun. It was taking a lot of patience to deal with her.

Instead, I sighed and said, "I know you've had a hard time. In hard times, you need a friend. I want to be that friend."

Bethany looked at me. Something seemed to crack in her hard outer shell.

"Okay. I'll give it a try," she said. "Let's go out for a swim."

We waded into the clear blue water of the Mexican coast. It splashed around our waists. Suddenly, I felt a jab.

"Ouch! That little blue jellyfish just stung me!"

We glanced around the water and saw the tiny blue bubbles of jellyfish to our right.

"I'm getting out, and I'm not *ever* coming back in," I said angrily.

Bethany took my arm. "Wait. You don't get to come to the beach very often. I can help you watch for them. They float on top of the water, so they're not that hard to see."

I smiled at Bethany. "You've got a deal."

We all want to be needed. Maybe what Bethany needed was someone to need her, to trust her. Maybe no one had ever done that before.

I was happy to be that someone. I was even happier that I had finally found the key to Bethany's heart!

Karen Cogan

Bossy Lara

"Bossy Lara, bossy Lara!" the class roared in chant. They kept on, getting louder and louder in their song.

My teacher, Ms. Dixon, sent me to sit in the corner for a while to quiet the class. I didn't understand at all. *I* knew how to operate the record player. *I* knew to be very careful when putting the needle down to not scratch the records. My father had taught me exactly what to do. And besides, not everyone had steady hands or the know-how to play a record without damaging it.

So why was it, I wondered, that the class got upset when I tried to take over and show Marcia how to handle the record player the right way? I was only trying to help, as I had done many times before. I also couldn't understand why the teacher had sent me to the corner. I was taught to always help my classmates if they didn't understand or know how to do something. If anything, I thought the class was wrong in their judgment of me. I thought the teacher was certainly wrong in siding with them.

When everyone was excused for recess, Ms. Dixon kept me in. I figured that I was in serious trouble, but I still didn't understand how my actions could have caused the teacher to react like this. I had never been in trouble this bad before.

"Why am I here and not at recess?" I asked Ms. Dixon.

The teacher didn't say a word. Instead, she placed a word puzzle in front of me. I guessed Ms. Dixon wanted me to do it, so I got out my pencil and attempted to solve it. This was like no other puzzle I had done before. It was difficult, with words I didn't understand. I raised my hand for help, but Ms. Dixon ignored me. Maybe Ms. Dixon was just keeping me in to protect me from the other students' mean words.

I struggled with the word puzzle until I was about to give up and throw it away. But I was not a quitter, and so I stayed with the challenge. Once I got one word, I was able to get another, and soon I had solved the problem by myself. I was so proud I did the puzzle on my own that I raised my hand high to get Ms. Dixon's attention.

Ms. Dixon walked over to me, picked up the finished puzzle, and smiled.

"I'm glad that you learned this important lesson from me."

I was confused. She hadn't done anything, hadn't

given me help in any way. Now she was taking the credit for my hard work!

Ms. Dixon wrote an "A" on my paper.

"Now perhaps you have learned to let other students make discoveries on their *own*. After all, *that* is the fun of learning."

Of course, she was right. And I finally understood how the others felt when I tried to take over and do things for them. I had taken away their chance to find out how good it feels when you figure things out by yourself.

In that moment, I decided that I would never do anything that would cause them to call me "Bossy Lara" ever again.

Lara Anderson

A Special Lunch

The best way to cheer yourself is to try to cheer someone else up.

Mark Twain

I could just barely climb up onto the kitchen counter, but that is where I was sitting, hungry and hopeful that our babysitter would make me something to eat. When she didn't answer my call, I dropped down and went to look for her. I found her asleep on the couch.

So I decided that I'd go find my sister, Ashley. She was coloring in her room. When she saw me, the first thing out of her mouth was, "I'm hungry. Let's make some sandwiches."

"I'll get the peanut butter 'cause you're too short!" I teased her.

"Yeah, but I'm stronger," she bragged.

We went into the kitchen, and I climbed back onto the counter and found the peanut butter in a cabinet up high. Ashley found the jelly in one of the lower cabinets.

"Give it to me," I demanded. I was hungry, so that made me kind of grumpy.

"You don't have to be so mean!" Ashley answered.

A second later, she said, "Hey, look!" Ashley had noticed that a bag of flour had broken and spilled on the floor of the cabinet.

"Mom's going to be mad, Ashley!" I said, accusing her of doing it.

Ashley threw a handful of flour at me for saying that.

"Hey!" I yelled, grabbing a handful of flour and throwing it at her.

We ran around the kitchen throwing flour at each other until we were white as ghosts. Flour floated in the air around us as we took off into the living room.

Suddenly, the grandfather clock on the wall started to ding.

"Oh, no! Mom's going to be home any minute!" I panicked. *What are we going to do about the mess?* I wondered nervously. It looked like it had snowed inside the house.

Ashley quickly ran and grabbed a vacuum, but she didn't know how to turn it on. Suddenly, the sound of keys jingled at the front door.

"Oh, no! Mom's home!" Ashley screamed. "We're going to get put in time-out for a whole hour!"

Mom walked in the door, tired from a long day at college. She took three steps into the house and shook her head.

Ashley and I ran to her with angel smiles on our faces. Mom didn't get mad at us, but she seemed kind of upset at the babysitter when she woke her up and showed her the mess we had made. Once the babysitter had gone, Mom went into her room.

"We're not in trouble!" I shouted with joy.

"Mom didn't look so good, Chris," Ashley said to me with a sad voice.

"What? She was smiling. Of *course* she looked good!" I assured her.

"Well, let's go see!" Ashley said, with a big-girl voice.

So we went to Mom's bedroom door and peeked in. Mom was sitting on her bed leaning over her homework. We noticed tears in her eyes.

"She's crying because we made such a mess!" Ashley whispered. "Come on. Let's go clean the house."

"Fine, but then she has to make us a sandwich!" I said.

"You're spoiled!" Ashley shot back. "Mom has to go to school on Saturdays after she has worked all week. And she has to go back to work tonight. She never gets a break."

So Ashley and I ran to the vacuum and finally found the button. I vacuumed, because I was stronger, no matter what Ashley said, and Ashley got a feather duster from the closet. Ashley dusted everything, even the VCR. Pretty soon, the flour was gone, and the floors were clean.

"I have an idea. Let's make a special lunch for Mom!" Ashley suggested.

"But *we're* the ones who are hungry!" I pouted.

"Stop being so selfish!" Ashley said. "Come on, I'm too short to get the peanut butter!"

"Fine," I said and walked into the kitchen with a frown.

I climbed up on the counter, and before long the two of us had made two sandwiches. Ashley got out some orange juice and poured a glass for Mom.

"I want to give the sandwiches to Mom!" I said.

"But then she'll think that you did everything!" Ashley said in a sad voice.

"Okay, you can give it to her. I'll give her the orange juice!" I agreed.

We took the meal to Mom, and she smiled.

"You made it for me? My kids made me lunch?" She was so happy she started to cry again.

"We cleaned the whole house, too!" Ashley bragged.

"I did all the vacuuming 'cause Ashley's not strong enough," I bragged.

Ashley stuck her tongue out at me for that.

"Well, thanks for all of your effort, but I'm only hungry enough for one sandwich. Who wants the other one?" Mom asked.

"Ashley, you can have it," I offered. But Ashley cut the sandwich in half, and we shared it.

"You two are the best kids I could ever ask for," Mom said as she got ready to go to work.

"No, you're the best mom!" we both said with a smile.

Seeing Mom happy made the peanut-butter-and-jelly sandwiches taste even better.

Christopher Geren

Throwing his coat over the mud puddle for the girls
seemed like a good idea at the time.

The Twenty-Dollar Bill

Nobody made a greater mistake than he who did nothing because he could do only a little.

Edmund Burke

When my mom and dad said that we could adopt a couple of kittens, I jumped at the chance to have some soft, cuddly animals around the house. So off we went to the Humane Society where there were a lot of animals up for adoption.

The first thing I noticed was that there was not a lot of room for the animals and not a lot of supplies to care for them. Even though they didn't have much, the people who worked there cared about the animals more than anything, and they did their best for them. Still, it seemed they had just barely enough food and medicine to keep the animals healthy.

When we started looking around, I saw a lot of animals

and fell in love with each of them. But my family and I finally settled on adopting two kittens we named Sox and Sierra. We went up to the front desk to sign the papers for them, and that's when I noticed a box on the counter. The Humane Society was hoping to get enough donations to buy more supplies for the animals and also build a new building to help even more abandoned animals.

We finished up and took our new kittens home, where they were sure to get a lot of love. Later that day, my mom and I went shopping, and as we were walking through the parking lot at the store, I noticed a green piece of paper three spaces away from our car. It was kind of wet, but it looked like it could be a dollar bill, so I walked over and picked it up. It wasn't a dollar bill—it was a twenty-dollar bill!

When I got home, I dried it off and thought about what to do with it. I considered spending it on a toy and a lot of other things. Right then, Sox climbed up into my lap, and I knew what I was going to do with the money.

I asked my mom to take me back to the Humane Society so that I could put the money in the donation box. The lady at the counter smiled and thanked me, and I felt really good about what I did.

If the Humane Society does raise enough money to build a new building, I will know that I helped many more animals that will come to live there one day—hopefully, only until someone comes along and lovingly adopts them like we did with Sox and Sierra.

Mallory McGinty, 10

Sometimes, Babies Get in the Way

When you carry out acts of kindness, you get a wonderful feeling inside. It is as though something inside your body responds and says, yes, this is how I ought to feel.

Harold Kushner

"A swing set! We have a swing set!" Six-year-old Sarah sprang out of bed. From her bedroom window, she could see the new addition in the back yard.

"Can I play on it right now?" she asked her mother.

"Sure," her mom said, and in an instant, Sarah was outside. She didn't even change out of her pajamas!

In the yard, Sarah checked out the new equipment; two swings, a slide, and a clubhouse. She was so busy she didn't notice that her mother had followed her outside.

"Dad and I know you'll be a wonderful big sister," her mother said, "so we wanted to get you something special. Besides, after the baby is born, we may not be able to go to the park as often as you'd like. Now you can play out here as much as you want."

Sarah's mother was going to have a baby any day now, and the doctor had told her to stay off her feet as much as possible. Sarah's father was spending more time at his office than usual, finishing up a big project so he could take time off when the baby came. That meant Sarah had to hang around the house a lot. She tried to keep herself busy by making decorations for the new baby's room. She'd spent hours making signs and drawings to welcome the new baby home. But now that she had a swing set, hanging around the house would be a lot more fun.

Later that week, the baby was born. Sarah had a new sister, and her name was Charlotte.

When Mom and Charlotte came home from the hospital, Sarah held her new sister in her lap, and Dad took pictures. Sarah showed Charlotte all the decorations she'd made for her room.

"I think it's time for Mom and Charlotte to rest now," said Dad. "Let's go out in the yard to give them some quiet."

Sarah was deciding whether to swing or slide first when she noticed something moving. At the base of the ladder, she saw a clump of dried grass. It was covering a small hole, and something in the hole was moving. She gently pushed the grass aside with her foot and was surprised to discover three baby rabbits!

Sarah replaced the grass that had been covering them and ran to tell her Dad.

"Dad! Dad! There are baby rabbits in the back yard! A mother rabbit had babies, just like Mom!"

Tugging him by the arm, she led him over to the ladder where the bunnies were hiding. It was then that Sarah realized she wouldn't be able to use the swing set without stepping in the hole.

"Great," she said. "Because of Charlotte, I can't play inside. And because of the bunnies, I can't play outside, either." It seemed like nothing was going right, and so Sarah began to cry.

"Hold on, hold on," said Dad. "There has to be a solution. I'm going to make a few calls."

Sarah waited outside until her dad came back.

"I called the nature center," he said. "They told me that I could use a big snow shovel to scoop up the bunnies and move them to a different spot."

"Then let's do it," said Sarah. "Let's move them someplace else."

"But," said Dad, "They also said that if I move the bunnies, there's a chance the mother rabbit won't want to take care of them anymore."

He headed to the garage to get the snow shovel. Sarah saw the bunnies moving around in the hole. What would they do without a mother to take care of them?

"Wait!" Sarah shouted. "Leave the bunnies where they are!"

"If I leave them there, you won't be able to play on the swing set. It may take a few weeks until they're ready to leave," Dad replied.

Sarah thought for a minute. She really wanted to play on her swing set, but . . .

"Dad, what if you and Mom came home from the hospital with our new baby, and our home wasn't here anymore? Where would we go? Where would we live? It would be terrible if it happened to us, so why should we do that to the rabbit family?"

As soon as Sarah said it, she knew she had made a good decision.

"You're absolutely right, honey," Dad said. "If it's okay with you, I'll leave them alone. How about if we take a walk to the park?"

"Maybe later, Dad," Sarah said. "I need to do something first!"

Sarah returned with a stack of paper and her crayons.

"What are you making?" Dad asked.

"I'm making a 'Welcome Home' sign," she said, "for the bunnies!"

Ruth B. Spiro

2

BEING A TEAM PLAYER

My hope for all people is simple, you see,
The simplest wish ever made by me.
My wish is for there to be peace everywhere,
And make everyone nice and everyone care.
The reason that I, a small little girl,
Want to have peace spread over the world,
Is just for one purpose, a good one I think,
So that people like you can smile and wink.
Ordinary people like you and I,
Or rich people in jets that can fly really high.
My simple wish, my hope and my dream,
Is that everyone would be part of one team.

Annie Loveless, 11

For the Love of Animals

How wonderful it is that nobody need wait a single moment before starting to improve the world.

Anne Frank

I have always loved animals. Even before I learned to write, when I watched TV specials that showed animals from around the world that needed help, I drew the shapes of the phone numbers you were asked to copy down from the screen. I would take what I had copied to my mother and tell her, "We need to call here. They need help. We need to help them."

For my fifth birthday party, instead of my friends bringing birthday gifts for me, my mom suggested that there was a way we could have my party help the animals in our community. We asked my friends to bring donations of cat and dog food that we could then give to a local animal shelter.

When I first saw the big pile of pet food, I was amazed. *Together, my friends and I can help an awful lot of animals,* I thought. *An awful lot.*

Afterward, when we went to the shelter, we told the volunteer, "We've brought some cat and dog food that we'd like to donate to the animals here. Could you open the back door so we don't have to bring it in through the main entrance?"

The shelter worker thought for a moment and then said, "Okay," but you could tell she thought opening the back door was unnecessary. She met us around back, and when we opened the van loaded with food, her mouth hung open.

"Wow! You sure do have pet food! What's all this?"

I told her my story about asking for pet food at my birthday party instead of presents, and she almost cried.

"You and your friends are so amazing! Thank you so very much from all of the animals, and for being so thoughtful and generous and kind." Her words made me feel very proud to realize that even as little kids, we could do something really important.

She let me go through the shelter and visit with all of the animals, holding kittens, and offering some of the treats I had brought to many of the others. It really made my heart fill with love and joy.

There was no doubt that I wanted to do the same thing again on my next birthday. Even though I didn't get all the presents that I might have gotten if I didn't ask for pet food, I really don't need more "stuff."

Besides, the feeling I get from doing this is better than any toy I might have gotten. And so I have done the same thing for each of my birthdays since then.

I just turned eleven, and I have been doing this for seven years and collected over 1,400 pounds of food for donation. I still feel very special each time I take that food to the shelter.

I started to think about other ways I could help besides just through my birthday parties, and I began selling lemonade at an art show. Soon, I added some of my own art—pictures of dogs and cats that I had painted. Many people bought them because they wanted to support my cause.

I also began making beaded bracelets that I called "Buddy Bracelets" because the money I made from them went to my animal buddies. I packaged them with a tag that explained what they were, and how by buying them people were helping the animals, and so anyone who received one as a gift would know that it was an extra-special bracelet.

I continue to make things to sell, and when people buy them, I love to tell how together we are helping the animals. When I am able to help the animals in the shelter, I am reminded of all the pets I have at home, my two dogs and one cat, my goats, and chickens. They are happy and healthy and safe and loved. They inspire me to continue to bring people together to help animals that aren't so lucky.

Emylee Cuthbertson, 11

Second Act

*E*verybody, my friend, everybody lives for something better to come. That's why we want to be considerate of every man—who knows what's in him, why he was born and what he can do?

Maxim Gorky

"We need Abraham Lincoln!" my third-grade teacher, Ms. Schlitter, announced to our class one morning. We were putting on a play about the month of February, and the narrator of the play was Abraham Lincoln, whose birthday falls on February 16. The narrator was the most important part of the play, and I was sure I would get it because I was the best speaker in class. Plus, I remembered things like facts, numbers, and stories, and I was a natural-born ham.

As I waited for Ms. Schlitter to call my name, I

glanced across the room at Charles Pender. Charles, or Slow-Poke Charlie as some of the kids called him, sat with a frown on his face. *Charles wouldn't be interested in our class play and being cast as Abraham Lincoln. Forget it! Charles can't remember anything. He's the most mixed-up kid I've ever seen. When he does remember to say something, it comes out so slow you can't understand him.*

Charles lifted his head and caught me looking at him. He waved in that shy way of his and reached for a book on his desk. *No, Charles couldn't be interested in our play.*

"Our Abraham Lincoln for the Month of February Play is Charles Pender!"

I couldn't believe my ears. I looked at Ms. Schlitter with shock on my face. Lots of kids in the room did. Even Slow-Poke Charlie raised his head and stared at her. He didn't look like he believed what she had just said.

"Ms. Schlitter," I heard myself say, "are you sure? Do you really want to cast Charles in the role?"

Ms. Schlitter went over to Charles and put a hand on his shoulder. "Charles will make a fine Abraham Lincoln," she told us, "as long as we support him."

I looked away from her. I knew everyone was probably looking at me, wondering what I had done to earn Ms. Schlitter's wrath. I didn't think the whole thing was fair. Then, a second unbelievable thing happened. Ms. Schlitter asked me to help Charles learn his lines for the play.

"What about me?" I asked. "Don't I get a part in the play?"

"You can be Charles' understudy," Ms. Schlitter told me. "If Charles gets sick and can't be at the play, you would take over the part of Abraham Lincoln."

At the mention of not being able to do the part, Charles raised his head. "You mean I don't have to be in the play?" he asked.

Ms. Schlitter patted his shoulder. "You'll make a great Lincoln, and I'm sure your parents will be proud."

"I guess," Charles said. "My mom would like it if I did. There are lots of lines."

"You'll help him learn his lines, won't you?" she asked me, giving me one of her 'I'm counting on you' looks.

Sighing, I nodded and tried not to scowl at Slow-Poke Charlie. "I'll help him."

Charles went back to reading his book.

The next day, I went over to his house. I'd never been to Charles' house before. I don't think anyone had, although he lived in the neighborhood. His slow-poke ways kept most of the kids from hanging out with him.

His mom let me in, and I dragged my feet to his room, wanting to be anywhere but there. I was about to knock on the door when I heard a cough. I listened, hoping there would be more, that Charles had caught a cold and wouldn't be in any shape to play his part. What I heard weren't more coughs, but singing. Charles was singing in his room!

I stood and listened, and found myself not believing

something for the third time that week. Charles could sing! He had a terrific voice, and sang loud and clear, not slowly at all. He didn't stumble or mumble. Then, I heard Charles switch from singing to saying lines from the play. He sounded great as Abraham Lincoln. He spoke in a strong voice and wasn't the least bit slow. I opened the door and went in his room.

"Wow!" I said. "That's pretty good."

"Hi," he said in a slow, low voice. "Do you want to help me learn these lines?"

"Sure," I said. "Why don't you start at the beginning?"

When Charles spoke, it was in the way I was used to hearing him speak. I caught him staring nervously at me. I understood everything in a flash. The only reason Charles was slow was because he was nervous. Nervous because he thought guys like me were staring at him, waiting to make fun of him. Even if I had never called him Slow-Poke Charlie aloud, I had thought of him that way just the same.

"Hey," I said when Charles had finished the first page of lines, "why don't we go out to the park and toss a ball? We can practice our lines and feed the ducks."

Charles looked straight into my eyes. "You really want to?"

"A good understudy takes care of the play's star," I told him. "And the way I heard you singing and saying your lines, we're going to have the best Abraham Lincoln our play has ever had."

I was right, too. During the play, I watched from

backstage as Charles delivered the performance of a lifetime. He and the class got a standing ovation. I wish I could have been out there with Charles, but when I saw the look on his face and heard all that applause, I realized that it was one of the best moments in both our lives.

John P. Buentello

Music Is Contagious

Music is as powerful as any medicine.
Oliver Sacks

"You know, Mom, I'd be more useful to you if I caught up on some of my chores," Emmy announced, thinking, *Then I can get out of going to the hospital.*

"Good try, but this time the chores can wait. Aunt Emelia is looking forward to seeing you," Emmy's mom answered as she put on her jacket.

Emmy didn't like hospitals. What was fun about seeing sick people, especially on a sunny Saturday in spring?

As she and her mom rode the hospital elevator up to the third floor, Emmy tried to take her mind off of the disturbing smell of hospital food mixed with ammonia that seemed to be climbing up with them. So she hummed one of the songs she would sing to her aunt. Although she had rehearsed the songs with her middle-school chorus over a hundred times, she was nervous about singing without the piano to help guide her.

The hallways were quiet, but as they neared Aunt Emelia's room, Emmy's thoughts were interrupted by the distant sound of laughter, maybe a boy's voice. She would have rather gone to that room. It sounded like a lot more fun. *Prepare to bite your fingernails, stare out the window, and nod a lot,* Emmy thought.

"Hello, Auntie Emelia!" Emmy's mom announced loudly as they entered the room.

Chuckling, Aunt Emelia said, "You're going to wake up the patients all the way down the hall. I've got my hearing aid on, Frannie." Then turning to Emmy, Aunt Emelia said, "Oh, Emmy, I'm so glad you've come, too."

"I miss your lasagna. When are you gonna go home, Aunt Emelia?" Emmy tried sounding cheerful as she leaned closer to give the old woman a kiss. Up until that moment, she hadn't realized how much she'd also missed that familiar perfume, as well being stamped on the cheek with her aunt's fire-engine-red lipstick. Aunt Emelia was trying to be her usual bubbly self, but Emmy could tell from her pale, drawn cheeks that the sickness had taken its toll.

"I knew you named her after me for a reason, Fran," she laughed. "And don't forget that you've promised to sing me some of your new tunes," she reminded Emmy. "But first, would you get me some coffee, sweetheart? Just turn left into the hall, and the machine's right next to the nurses' station."

Good ol' Aunt Emelia hasn't forgotten how to give out orders, thought Emmy. Still, there was something comforting about it, like things were almost back to normal.

" . . . and come right back!" her mom yelled, as Emmy walked out.

Emmy wandered past endless carts piled with all sorts of packaged tubes, needles, trays, and bandages. As she walked on, she noticed the distant sound of music and wondered where it was coming from.

While she waited for the coffee machine to fill the second cup, the music stopped. Instead, a loud voice came from that direction. Emmy left the cups of coffee on the table and followed the voice. Then the music started up again, and Emmy found the room from where the music was coming. As she peeked inside, she was surprised to hear, "Come on in!" A boy who appeared to be about her age welcomed her. He was thin, but seemed to have lots of energy.

Emmy quickly noticed that the only other bed in the room was vacant, so she asked curiously, "Who have you been talking to?"

"Oh, lately, I talk to myself while I write. It's been kind of lonely since my roommate went home." He pointed at the other bed. "And TV bores me. . . . By the way, I'm Richard. Don't worry, I'm not contagious," he added.

"I'm Emmy," she giggled.

Emmy glanced down at her watch as she sat down on the empty bed, and the boy told her about his medical problems.

"It'll act up off and on for the rest of my life," Richard explained. "But when I'm feeling good, I play just as hard as any other kid. It's not so bad," he assured her.

Emmy admired his good attitude. She could not imagine being in a hospital room for two days, let alone two weeks, away from her friends and activities.

"If it weren't for this little keyboard, I would've gone crazy here," Richard said, adding proudly, "I write my own music."

Emmy looked down to the floor at his electronic keyboard and was struck with an idea.

"Can you play by ear?" Emmy asked.

"Singing? Forget about it, but playing . . . you name it," Richard answered. "But why?"

"Well, do you think the nurses would let you walk to my aunt's room with me?" Emmy asked.

"Sure. I'm probably going home tomorrow. I can walk around. Why?" Richard asked.

Just then, a loud voice suddenly announced, "Would Emmy Delcora please return to Room 309?"

Emmy's mouth dropped open. "Oh, no, that's me!"

Looking down at her watch, she realized that almost an hour had passed since she had left Aunt Emelia's room.

"I must've lost track of time. My mom's probably worried sick and mad at me! Let's get going, Richard. My aunt's waiting for me to sing, and . . . you're my accompanist!"

Richard's eyes opened wide. "Just point the way!"

he said as he threw on his robe, tucked the keyboard under his arm, and scurried down the hall after Emmy.

When they entered her aunt's room, her mom asked anxiously, "Where have you been, young lady?"

Aunt Emelia joked, "That's the longest I've ever had to wait for a cup of coffee, and instead, she brings back a new friend!"

"I'm sorry I made you worry, but I found a piano player. Mom, Aunt Emelia, this is Richard."

Emmy never had so much fun singing her songs as she did that day. Richard made a perfect accompanist. Just as they finished, they heard applause and turned around to see an audience of patients and nurses crowded around Aunt Emelia's door. Emmy was beaming. It felt good to see so many people enjoying their music.

As she and her mom prepared to leave, Emmy turned to Richard and said, "Thanks for saving the day!"

"Thanks for making mine!" he answered, and they promised to keep in touch.

From then on, Emmy thought of hospitals a little differently. She realized that fun is where you find it. And even sick people—*especially* sick people—need to have fun.

Mary Lou DeCaprio

Standing Up

Courage is simply the willingness to be afraid and act anyway.

Robert Anthony

When I was ten years old, I spent two weeks at a girls' summer camp where it rained every day. I remember cleaning the outhouses and having to live with the spiders, mosquitoes, ticks, and muddy trails. The tents weren't bad, though. They had wood floors and a canvas top, and four to six kids slept in each of them.

My favorite times were the rainy nights when my roommates and I would read and write letters. Our favorite thing to do was make shadow shows with our flashlights on the tent walls until the camp counselors would suddenly open the cabin door, scare us to death, and then tell us to go to sleep.

One evening at dinner, they made all of the kids eat

a piece of meat they pretended was "pig intestines." I hid mine in my napkin, but got caught, so the counselors made me eat it right in front of them. I gagged because it really smelled bad, and it tasted as bad as it smelled.

I'll always remember the evening of the ice-cream social with the boys' camp across the lake.

After dinner, when some poor girl threw her chicken bones into the paper basket, the camp counselors got mad. They told us that no one was going to have ice cream until the person who threw the chicken in the paper basket stood up and admitted her mistake. No one said a thing.

Then one of the counselors said, "Okay. We'll close our eyes, along with everyone else. Whoever put the chicken in the paper basket can go take it out and put it into the correct trash can. We won't say a thing, and then we can all have ice cream."

We all closed our eyes three times, but all three times, nobody moved. On the fourth round of closing our eyes, the counselors started talking about canceling the ice-cream social. That's when I thought to myself, *This is ridiculous. Somebody has to do something. They can't take our ice-cream social away. That's not fair!*

Even though I wasn't the one who threw the chicken in the basket, I felt sorry for whoever did and how scared she must have been.

"Okay, everyone . . . one more time. Close your eyes, and we'll slowly count to ten," the counselors yelled out. Everyone closed their eyes.

That's when I made my move. I slowly opened my eyes, and quickly and quietly tiptoed to the paper basket. I pulled out the chicken bones. Suddenly, I heard the counselors speed up their counting, " . . . 5, 6, 7, 8, 9, 10." They opened their eyes and shouted, "Ah, ha!"

I was so scared. I told them that I hadn't been the one who put the chicken in the paper basket.

"Then why did you take the chicken *out* of the paper basket?" they asked.

"Because . . . I wanted everyone to have ice cream," I cried.

The counselors pointed out to all the other girls how good I was, and therefore, I would be the only one allowed to have ice cream. That made me feel *really* bad, so I stood where I was with my feet together and my arms crossed. "If the rest of the troop can't have ice cream, then I don't want any either," I said.

The counselors eventually gave in and let all of the kids have ice cream. I was amazed.

To this day, I still don't know what made me do that. Maybe, deep down inside, I knew even then there are times when kids need to stand up for each other.

Christine Mix

NO RODEO®

Reprinted by permission of Robert Berardi. ©2007 Robert Berardi.

Someone to Count On

*If we survive danger, it steels our courage
more than anything else.*

Reinhold Niebuhr

As the littlest of the Stubbs Street kids, I always had
to run to keep up. If someone said, "Let's go to the
mangroves," I'd jump up right away, ready to run.
Then off we'd go, my short legs moving fast. There
were two ways to get there: over the bridge or
through the swamp. We always went through the
swamp.

Whatever the kids said, I agreed with them. It was
better than staying at home. Anyone who stayed
home was a baby.

Tom's big brother, Sam, hung around with us sometimes. Sam was older than all of us and had a job. We
thought he was rich.

One day when Sam was with us, someone suggested

that we all go to the brick pit. I got up so quickly that I was in front of everyone. We went through the scrub and up a bit of a hill. After a while, I was at the back, and Sam was in front.

The brick pit was a deep hole in the ground. A fence made from metal sheets wrapped around it. Signs were everywhere that said KEEP OUT, but we could get in at a couple of places where the sheets had been pulled apart. I know we shouldn't have gone in there. Our parents always told us not to go to the brick pit. But I was little then, and I did what everyone else did.

We always went close to the edge, threw stones into the pit, and waited for them to hit the bottom. The sides were so steep we couldn't see all the way down. We had to listen until we heard them hit. This, time we were all throwing, but nobody heard anything.

"There might be some water in it," Sam said. He walked past me over to the right and said, "I'm going over there. It's a bit higher, and I might be able to see the bottom."

The soil was loose, and a bush had its roots in the air, like it had been ripped out. That's when I heard myself shouting. "No, it's dangerous! The dirt's falling in."

Sam looked around. All the kids looked at me. It felt strange. Usually I didn't say anything, and now I was shouting madly.

"It's falling in," I said a bit more quietly.

Sam looked back to where he was going to walk and said, "No, it isn't."

So all the kids said, "No, it isn't."

Sam walked on to the ground—and vanished! The soil simply fell away under his weight, taking him and the big bush with it. I remember hearing Gavin scream like a girl. I'd never heard him make a noise like that before. Then he turned and ran away from the edge. All the other kids were pushing past him to see what had happened.

"Sam's gone!" he kept calling out.

But Sam was still there. He was hanging on to the roots of a big tree. I saw rocks and soil bumping down the slope beneath him and over the pit edge. He was covered in dirt and grass. But he was strong and lifted his knees up to get a better grip on the root. Then he moved his hands and his elbow and got a better hold. And that was how he climbed back up to the top. I noticed that he was shaking and, for a moment, I thought he was crying, but he wasn't. This was the only time I ever saw Sam look scared.

We all walked back home, and no one said a word.

But on that silent walk, new and different thoughts ran through my head. *I* was the only one who had seen the trouble ahead. Nobody, not even Sam, had been able to do what I did. And that surprised me.

I could tell that the other boys were looking at me differently—as if I was someone to count on, as if I were, finally, really part of the group. Tom even put his hand on my shoulder as we walked along.

A few weeks later, one of the kids said, "Let's go to the brick pit." A couple of other kids stood up.

I knew it was deadly dangerous at the pit, and I didn't want any of them to get hurt or killed.

"No," I said. "Let's go to the mangroves."

So we went to the mangroves instead.

Richard Brookton

The Gravel Pit

The family is one of nature's masterpieces.
George Santayana

The station wagon was full of kids: my brothers and sisters, plus a few neighborhood kids, all squished together on the seats.

"Ouch!" My little brother's sharp elbow poked me in the eye. The tall girl from next door pushed against me to make room by the window for my older sister. It was like being in a basket full of puppies. Everyone wiggled and squirmed, making as much noise as possible.

"The curse of a big family," I mumbled to myself. "It's a terrible, terrible curse."

"Renee's saying bad stuff!" yelled one of my brothers, the one with the sharp elbow.

"Renee . . ." my mom called out. "Please! Just try to get along."

"Okay," I mumbled a little louder. "But tell him to quit stabbing with his elbow."

"Are we there yet?" shouted my baby sister.

Mom smiled. I rolled my eyes. Being part of a big family was really starting to bug me. People banging on the bathroom door all the time. People eating all the snacks in the house. People jumping in the front seat first, so I always had to sit in the back. What was a kid supposed to do?

I need a break, I thought as I scratched an old scab on my knee. *What I wouldn't give to be an only child—just once.* But I knew there was no chance of that. I bounced and bumped as the crowded family station wagon rolled down the small road.

"The gravel pit is about three minutes away," my mom said cheerfully. "You'll have plenty of time to swim."

Swimming. At least that was a peaceful activity. I could float on my back and look at the sky. I could pretend that I was the only person in the world. At least I *could* float on my back. It was the only way I knew how to swim.

Mom steered the car off the road and parked carefully beside a small row of cars.

"One at a time . . ." she yelled before the car doors opened. "No one gets trampled."

Nobody listened. The station wagon was like a boxcar full of monkeys. All the doors flew open at once. Hands and feet and a few heads shot out of each door in a tangled mess.

"Hey!" "Watch it!" "No fair!" After pushing, shoving, and whining, we finally all tumbled out.

I quickly pulled off my jeans, T-shirt, socks, and flip-flops, and finally got down to my faded swimsuit.

"Yeehaa!" I yelled as I splashed into the gravel pit. Cold water stung my face. I dunked my head under the water, and it shot up my nose. After standing up again, I sniffed and snorted. Then I dropped backward into the water and began to float. The water sat around my ears, smooth and silent. The sun warmed my face. I was a leaf floating in a large gravel-pit puddle. No pushing. No yelling. Everything was silent under water. No crazy mix of neighbor kids and family kids. For the moment, I was an only child.

Yeah, I thought, *an only child. More presents at Christmas. More treats at the grocery store. I could sit in the front seat all the way home from the store. No more tall stacks of dishes to wash at supper.* My stomach growled at the thought of food. Hadn't Mom packed a huge bag of chips and a jug of iced tea for our snack?

I stood up to wade to shore.

Gulp! Dark sandy water suddenly filled my mouth and covered my head. The rocky ground was gone.

Shoosh! I tried to kick to the surface. As my face peeked out of the water, I took a deep breath. Splashing and twisting, I tried to swim. It didn't work. I only knew how to float. And I only knew how to start floating in shallow water.

The water closed over my head again. I thought about my mom. *Where was she? What would she do if she* couldn't find me? *What about my brothers and sisters?* As a hundred thoughts bounced through my head, I rose back to the top of the water. This time I didn't try to take a deep breath.

"*Ahhhh!*" I screamed after a quick gasp. Then I sank back down into the dark water. My head filled with pictures of my family. Everyone was crying. It was like a movie in a theater, except I was under water. Everyone missed me. They were so sad . . . so . . .

Shoosh! I felt the water swirling around me. Something warm and strong touched my hand. *A shark in a gravel pit?* No . . . it was someone's hand.

I couldn't see, but I could feel my body moving as the hand started to pull me through the water. It pulled and pulled until I could feel gravel under my feet, and I stumbled onto shore. My legs folded under me like thin pieces of construction paper.

"We did it!" yelled one of my brothers as I looked up and saw my mother holding my hand.

"It was sooo cool," cried another kid. "We walked right into the deep part. . . . The water was so deep. . . ."

Another kid started talking at the same time. "Yeah, we all held hands and made a human chain so Mom could get Renee."

I was speechless. Kids ran all around me, jumping, running, yelling, screaming. What could I say? Maybe this great big crazy family wasn't so crazy. After all, they were the human chain. Because of them, I was on dry ground—right where I wanted to be.

Renee Hixson

Adam Gets to Play

The other sports are just sports. Baseball is a love.

Bryant Gumbel

Early spring always brings out Adam's baseball fever. My son's love for the game even outdoes his love for his bike. This spring he was more excited than ever because he was old enough to try out for Little League. Getting on the league meant one very important thing: practice.

Adam wanted to be a pitcher. He did not want to try out for any other position. So, with his father as his trainer and a new glove, he set out to achieve his goal. Every evening and weekend, they practiced together: pitching, working the strike zones, catching, and batting.

At first, Adam had trouble with his swing, and his father gave him pointers on how he should grip and position the bat, and where to stand in the batter's box. When his father pitched to him, Adam worked on tightening up his strike zone. When it came time to work on his pitching, Adam's father would be the catcher. Working on the batter's strike zone, Adam pitched high balls and low balls. He caught the ball when his father threw it back, and then he would pitch again.

On the day of the first team practice, the children and their parents met at the ball field. The coach called out names and positions for the first tryouts. As the game progressed, the players switched different positions while the coaches watched. Adam moved through the field positions, taking his turn at batting, catching, and pitching. At the end of the practice, the coach called the team, and the children formed a circle around him. He called out each of their names and told them the positions they would play. As the coach assigned positions, the circle of children grew smaller, as one by one they left to return to their parents. Their cheerful voices filled the air as they told their parents what positions they'd been given.

Adam approached our family while we were packing up our lawn chairs, getting ready to go home. He looked upset as he grabbed a chair and carried it to the car.

"So?" his father asked. "What position did you get? You played well out there."

Adam couldn't hide the disappointment in his voice when he told his father that the coach had assigned him the catcher's position.

"That's great! You don't know how lucky you are. You get to play every game," his father encouraged him. "Pitchers get tired, and when they do, sometimes they can't even seem to get the ball over the plate. That's why there are relief pitchers. But catchers play all the time. You'll always have action at the plate—tagging out runners as they come in for a run, catching pop-up foul balls . . . the coach must think highly of your catching skills."

As Adam's father talked up the catcher's position, the pride he felt for his son shone through. He told Adam how on a team, each person is placed in the position he can play best based on his strengths. "That's what makes a team strong," he assured Adam.

Adam played catcher for that first year, and every year after that. But he never quit working on his pitching skills. He'd still love to play that position, and some day he might. But for now, he's happy because he gets to play in every game.

Talia Haven

Swimming on a Goat

Energy and persistence conquer all things.

Benjamin Franklin

Eva knew she would have to swim on the goat again. The thought made her want to turn her bicycle around and head home, but she didn't. She kept pedaling along the river's edge toward Mr. Kovar's house for her swimming lesson.

Eva's town had no public pools. The university had a pool, but it was only for special swim teams. Eva had seen the pool when her older brothers had been on the school swim team, and she longed to swim in its shimmering blue water.

But for now, Eva and the other students had to learn to swim by lying on a piece of plywood nailed on a sawhorse. Eva thought it looked like a goat.

When she reached Mr. Kovar's house, he was waiting for her. He wore his usual frown.

"Front crawl. One hundred strokes," he said.

Eva climbed onto the sawhorse and lay on her stomach.

Mr. Kovar walked in a circle around Eva as she practiced her strokes.

"Fingers together and point your toes," he said as he motioned with his wooden pointer. If one of Eva's arms or legs began to lag, he tapped the lazy limb. "A swimmer does not slap the water," he said, tapping her arm. "A swimmer slices the water. A swimmer is precise."

Eva wanted to remind him there was no water, but she didn't.

Next he tapped her head. "You will breathe only when you turn your head."

Eva peeked at Mr. Kovar when she turned her head. He scowled as he watched every finger, every toe, and every muscle. Would she ever be able to please him?

"Thirty-seven, thirty-eight," he counted, never losing track.

Week after week, Mr. Kovar counted and tapped, tapped and counted.

Eva decided to try and think of things that would make her lessons fun. One week, she imagined she was swimming across the ocean with dolphins. The next week, she pretended she was shipwrecked and had to swim to the rescue boat.

She also kept track of how many times Mr. Kovar tapped her. Each week, she tried to break her record for fewest taps.

One day, Mr. Kovar said, "You are ready to swim in the water."

Eva smiled. "The university pool!"

Mr. Kovar frowned. "You cannot swim in the pool unless you are on a team. You cannot be on a team unless you pass my class. And I cannot pass you until I see you swim in the water. You must swim in the river."

"The river?" Eva gasped. "Is it safe?"

The river was cold, muddy, and smelled like a garbage bin. No one swam in that river unless it was by accident.

"It is safe if you are a good swimmer," said her teacher. "And if you take a long bath afterward."

On the day of the swim, Eva and her mother met Mr. Kovar at the river. When Mr. Kovar gave the signal, Eva rushed into the brown water. The chill almost took her breath away, but it also made her move quickly.

This was nothing like swimming on the goat. And yet, her muscles knew exactly what to do. She remembered the strokes she had learned in her lessons. She pulled with her hands. She kicked with her feet. She turned her head to breathe. Without practicing so many hours on the goat, she never would have been strong enough to swim in the river.

Eva felt strong and swift, like a dolphin. And for the first time, the strokes made sense. She moved faster when her fingers were together. Her kick felt stronger when she pointed her toes. Her strokes had more power when she did what she had been taught to do.

Mr. Kovar motioned for Eva to swim back to shore. He was smiling!

Mom wrapped Eva in a towel. Eva's teeth chattered.

Mr. Kovar clasped his hands behind his back and looked down at Eva. "You would be surprised how many of my students quit. They hate swimming on the sawhorse."

You mean the old goat, Eva thought as she tried to look surprised.

"They do?"

"Yes, but not you," Mr. Kovar said. "You have done very well. I will speak to the coach, and you'll practice with the swim team next week . . . at the university pool."

Eva's wide smile made her teeth chatter more loudly. But she didn't mind.

Lana Krumwiede

The Gift Givers Club

For it is in giving that we receive.

St. Francis of Assisi

One day, I was Rollerblading in our yard with my sister Alison, when some kids we'd never seen before came up the road toward our house. Because we were just about the only kids in our neighborhood, we skated over to greet them. That's when we noticed that they were all about our ages. So we asked their names, and as they told us. They also mentioned they had just moved into the neighborhood.

Ashley was a year younger than me. Jessica was a year younger than my sister Alison, and they had two younger brothers.

After we met and played for a while, they went home. Soon we realized we had forgotten to ask exactly where they lived. So the next day after school, we went around our big neighborhood in search of "the new neighbor kids."

For two days, we rode our bikes looking for any sign of them. Finally, on the third day, Alison found them.

"Kendal!" she announced through a walkie-talkie. "It's the yellow house on the street behind ours!" I hurried and met up with Alison. We rang the doorbell and waited.

"Hello," their mother said as she opened the door.

"My name is Kendal. . . ."

"I'm Alison. . . ."

"We met your kids while they were biking up the road past our house."

"We were wondering . . . um . . . can they come out and play for a while?" we asked.

"Sure!" she answered. "Kids! Some friends are here to see you!"

We played for hours that day, and within a week we were best friends with their family.

One day, as we were out playing, Ashley suggested that we start a club called "The Gift Givers." Ashley is full of kindness, so we weren't surprised when she thought of this. As members of the club, we would give up things we loved and leave them on the porch of a neighbor's home. After ringing the doorbell, we would hide long enough to watch the surprised look on their faces, and then we'd be off to other homes to do the same thing again.

One day, I answered the telephone at my house,

and on the other end was an older woman I recognized from our neighborhood. We had just delivered a gift to her house.

"Are you a member of The Gift Givers?" she asked.

"Yes, I'm a member," I answered, trying to sound serious.

"I am a neighbor of yours, and I just received a lovely gift and a beautiful poem with the last words, 'God bless you.'" She sounded happy, yet sad. "Your gift was the perfect thing to cheer me up because it is something that I needed but couldn't afford to pay for myself. My husband is dying from cancer, so to me, your gesture *was* a blessing from God. So I just wanted to call and say thank you to you and your club members, and God bless you, too."

"We are all very happy that it helped you," I answered. "Is there anything else we can do?"

"You can pray for my husband, please. He's very sick," the old woman replied.

"We will," I assured her, and then we hung up.

For the next three months, the members of The Gift Givers Club made a lot of people in our neighborhood happy as we continued to do nice things for them. But our club came to an end when our wonderful new friends moved to California.

Although our friends are no longer here with us, the memories we made being together in The Gift Givers Club will remain in our hearts forever.

Kendal Kornacki, 13, and *Alison Kornacki, 9*

3

BEING RESPONSIBLE

Have you heard of responsibility?
It's such a big word
But there's not a lot to it
Haven't you heard?
It's when you do something
Without being asked.
It might seem hard,
But it's not a difficult task.
You might forget to follow through.
You might want to mess around.
But to be responsible
You've got to buckle down.
Do what you're told
Don't make Mom count to three
Because everyone needs
To take responsibility.

Nicole Rinaldi, 13

Who Let the Dogs Out?

It's always helpful to learn from your mistakes because then your mistakes seem worthwhile.

Garry Marshall

Every summer, Jim, Marsha, and I spent at least two fun-filled weeks with Aunt Erma, my mother's older sister, and Uncle Leonard at their home in Madison, Wisconsin.

Uncle Leonard owned hunting dogs: six or so at any given time, usually beagles or Labradors. Marsha, Jim, and I were dog people. To us, dogs were part of the family. They lived in the house, ate, slept, and played with you like a friend. They may even learn tricks. After all, our dog, Chip, back home did. One summer, we discovered that this wasn't the case with Uncle Leonard's hunting dogs.

Diamond and Valarie, yellow Labradors, were mother

and father to five puppies. They lived outside in fenced doghouses with runs where they could exercise. Diamond lived in one pen, and Valarie and the pups lived in another pen all year, even during the winter.

"Don't they get cold?" I asked Uncle Leonard.

"If dogs live inside, they get spoiled and can't do their work," he replied, which didn't answer my question about being cold. I figured that outside dogs must be stronger and tougher than inside dogs. After all, they earned their keep by being good hunting dogs. "Hunting dogs are not for child's play," Uncle Leonard used to tell us.

But we felt sorry for the dogs. They never got to enjoy being inside with people. So one day, we let them come inside. It was Jim's idea. We wanted to give them a nice afternoon playing in the house, away from the heat and the flies.

"Come on," he said. "Uncle Leonard won't mind."

Valarie walked in first and began sniffing around curiously. She was no problem at all. But as soon as Diamond entered the house, he immediately began to "mark his territory." That meant he peed on the legs of every piece of furniture in the house. We were amazed by how big this dog's bladder must be (and I guess it was full) because even though he left his mark everywhere, there seemed to be plenty to go around. First, he hit the dining-room table, then the chair next to the sofa, the coffee table, and whatever else he could leave a few droplets on as we chased him from room to room.

"You go left, and I'll go right," Jim said. "Maybe we can corner him in the kitchen."

Marsha, our little sister, just sat on the sofa laughing hysterically as Jim and I chased him through the house. We learned that Diamond was really good at tag (which he decided we were playing). As we slipped on every throw rug in the house, we were fortunate that nothing was destroyed in the process. Nothing was truly damaged except our pride.

"Here comes Uncle Leonard!" Marsha cried.

That was the first and last time we saw Uncle Leonard get really mad at us. "What in the world have you kids done?" he demanded.

He mumbled under his breath as he walked to the garage and returned with two pails, a mop, and several rags. True to his gentle nature, though, he didn't tell Aunt Erma on us. She would have punished us big time. He just made us clean every speck of pee on the floor and furniture, and figured that the clean-up was punishment enough.

We wiped and mopped for over an hour. Every chair leg had to be disinfected. Aunt Erma never knew what we had done. When she returned home, she sniffed the air and casually asked, "Why do you kids smell like Lysol?" We just shrugged our shoulders and ran quickly out of the back door.

Arlene Y. Burke

My Very Own Dog

You are never given a dream without also being given the power to make it true. You may have to work for it, however.

Richard Bach

My very own dog. I can have my very own dog? These thoughts were swirling in my head as I stared at the black-and-white print of the newspaper ad:

> **DOG TO GIVE AWAY.**
> **LAB AND COLLIE MIX.**
> **GOOD WITH KIDS.**

I had begged and begged my parents for a dog.
"Come on, Dad! Our yard is huge. I'll take care of it," I pleaded. "I will!"

Up until then, his only response had been, "We'll see."

My hopes had always hung on the edge of a cliff, ready to go crashing down. But this was the day that my hopes soared to the sun. My dad had pointed out the ad to me; he made the phone call; he drove us in the van across town to pick up the dog. All the while, I was thinking, *My very own dog, my very own dog.* Visions of a peaceful dog sleeping next to me danced in my mind.

"Her name is Grace," the owner told us. "She's good, but she barks at the traffic." She sighed.

I nodded, barely hiding my excitement. When I grasped Grace's leash, it tingled in my fingers. Her pink tongue lolled out as she panted heavily. "It's okay, girl," I soothed her. I rubbed her golden fur and traced the thick black stripe down her back with my fingers.

"It's okay. We'll be home soon." Grace looked at me with untrusting brown eyes.

Dad pulled into our driveway. I swung the side door open, and Grace took off like a rocket. I had a firm grip on the leash . . . or so I thought. It snapped, letting Grace free. My very own dog raced down our sloping backyard, under the white picket fence, and into our neighbor's yard. She circled that yard once and slipped back to ours.

"Grace! Grace!" I yelled. "Come back here!"

I screamed her name repeatedly. Dad called her. Mom joined in the chorus. We begged. We pleaded.

But our voices meant nothing to *my very own dog.*

Dad looked at me. "She's your dog. She's your responsibility. You'll need to figure out how to get her back."

"I don't want her back!" I yelled in frustration. "How can I have a dog if she won't listen? I can't do it!" A big tear rolled down my cheek.

"Try some food," Dad suggested.

I set out a pan of cool water and some fresh dog food. "Grace . . . Grace!" I kept yelling, even as my voice went hoarse. Grace paced along our side of the picket fence. Finally, she slinked up to lap the water. The moment I stepped toward her, leash in hand, she bounded away.

"Grace!" I stomped my foot.

My very own dog . . . my dreams of petting her . . . of feeding her . . . of playing with her . . . were running away. I finally sat on the grass and watched her pace. *What if I never caught her? What if she bolted into the road and a truck ran over her?* My tears of anger became tears of concern.

Just then, Grace bounded past me, across our driveway, and into another neighbor's yard—the one with the cat.

"Oh, no," I groaned. I followed her as fast as I could. I noticed Mary-Jo standing in front of her house. I waved halfheartedly.

"Is that your dog?" Mary-Jo asked.

I could feel red creeping into my face. *My very own dog.*

"Yes."

"I think she likes Peter," she replied.

I turned to see Mary-Jo's husband sitting on the grass with his hand extended toward Grace. He had a rope in his other hand. His voice was soothing—like hot chocolate. "Come here, girl . . . come here." Grace hesitated before creeping closer, her head tucked to the ground. She nudged his hand. He rubbed her behind her ears. Unnoticed by *my very own dog,* Peter slipped the rope around her head.

"Amazing," I said.

Peter smiled. "Just use a little gentleness and a quiet voice." He handed me the rope.

"Thanks," I said. "Sorry for your trouble."

"No problem," Mary-Jo said. "Enjoy your new dog."

As I tied Grace to the tree in front of our house, she looked at me with sad brown eyes. She seemed to be apologizing. I crept closer to her, my fingers snuggling into her fur. She nudged me.

I sat down next to her to enjoy her company. It *was* just like my dream. Nothing was in our way now. I could handle Grace—no problem.

"Promise you won't run away again?" I whispered. She blinked.

"I guess if you do, we'll have Peter to help," I said.

I wasn't sure, but I think she nodded her head in agreement. So I hugged *my very own dog* for the very first time.

Kathleen Bracher

Who's to Blame?

It was a very exciting day for my sister and me. As soon as our dad got home, he was going to give us a special gift. We had our eyes peeled open on that beautiful sunny day as we looked out the front door, waiting to see my dad come through it, bearing gifts. It wasn't our birthday or anything; our dad had just felt like getting us something special.

The car pulled up, and Dad got out carrying a large bag. He walked up to the door and handed us the bag before he even got inside. Mindy and I looked into the bag together and pulled out the most beautiful red purses we'd ever seen, one for Mindy and one for me.

"I love it!" I said, as I gave my dad a big kiss. Mindy did the same. Mindy always copied me.

We had our new purses, but they were empty. Mindy wanted to put something in them—something exciting. So we looked around the house to see what we could find. We couldn't find much until we walked into our mom and dad's bedroom. I looked inside one of Dad's dresser drawers and found what looked like a ton of money.

"Mindy, look what I found!"

She came running, "What, what is it?"

I pointed inside the drawer. "Look . . . it's money. We can stick all this money inside our new red purses."

Mindy looked confused. "That's mom and dad's money. We can't take that."

I started to put the money into my purse, and Mindy copied me. Our purses were as stuffed as could be. We ran out of our parents' room and headed for ours.

"Let's hide our purses in our dresser drawer," I said. As soon as we did this, I heard a loud yell—and we never heard yelling in our house.

"Honey, our money is missing," my mother shouted. My dad was frantic, and I could hear him pacing downstairs. "I know I put the money in our drawer. Where could it be?"

I heard footsteps coming up the stairs toward our room. Soon, both our parents were standing in front of us.

"Did you happen to find some money?" my father asked.

Mindy looked at me with fear in her eyes. "No," I said.

Dad and Mom stood there waiting for another answer. Mindy and I both became nervous.

"Where are your new red purses?" my mother asked. "Can I see them?"

I walked over to our dresser and started to pull them out. Mindy began to cry. "It was Michelle's idea. It's all her fault. She made me do it."

I handed Mom the purses. She looked inside, and there was all of the money.

"It was Mindy's fault. She wanted to find something extra special to stick into her purse."

My parents sat us down and talked about the importance of taking responsibility. "It doesn't matter whose fault it is. You have to live up to your own actions," Mom said. "Now, it doesn't matter whose bright idea this was. You both are responsible for doing something that you shouldn't have. You are both lucky that we found the money," my father added.

Mindy and I apologized to them and to each other, and gave our parents a tight hug. We realized they were right, and that we should never blame each other for our own choices.

"What *can* we stick in our purses?" Mindy asked. Suddenly, she ran for the Monopoly money. I wasn't going to stick *that* in my purse. I put some stickers, lip gloss, and candy in mine.

And, yes, Mindy copied me.

Michelle Rossi

Following the Rules

Don't learn safety rules simply by accident.

Anonymous

It was just before dinnertime, and the smell of burning leaves filled the October air. A large crowd of people gathered across the far end of the street to watch the fall of a gigantic tree that was being taken down in my neighborhood. This was no easy task. I watched from the cement steps of my house as the tree, bound with heavy ropes and chains, was lowered to the sidewalk.

Soon, the once gigantic tree was now without limbs or leaves, and it fell safely to the ground with a muffled, "Thud!"

But the kids and grown-ups did not leave. They moved in closer to linger around this wonderful old tree. Like them, I wanted to run my hands on the tree's bumpy bark and say good-bye, but I was only

five years old and wasn't allowed to cross the busy
city street.

But as I became more sad watching the tree nearly
disappear, I thought to myself, *What's the worst thing
that could happen?*

I didn't see any cars coming, so I ran across the street
to say good-bye to the fallen tree. After what seemed
like a short while of standing around and talking with
some of the people who were also sad to see the tree be
cut down, a sinking feeling grew in my stomach. I realized that I had stayed too long. *I am late for dinner, and
I'm in trouble,* I thought. Without even thinking, and
without looking to see if there were any cars coming, I
darted out between two parked cars and raced toward
my side of the street. I barely heard the screech of tires
before a car struck me down. One of my shoes flew into
the gutter. The car passed over my body, and I was
covered with grease, bruises, and blood.

In what seemed like only seconds since the accident happened, my father was standing above me. He
leaned over and looked into my eyes as he said, "Joe—
I love you, son—the ambulance is on its way."

At the hospital, it was discovered that I was not
seriously injured. While the car drove over my body,
the wheels never touched me. It was a miracle I have
never forgotten. I was grateful to be alive and very
surprised to have only some minor bruises.

My tearful parents hugged me and reminded me
that I wasn't supposed to cross the street by myself,
and that I should always look in both directions for

cars before taking one step into a street. They also told me that I should use crosswalks when walking across a street. As I got older, I realized even more how not all kids are so lucky when they break safety rules.

I learned the hard way that day to respect the rules my parents set and to be more responsible. And from then on, it was obvious to me that following the rules was simply a smart thing to do.

Joseph Sottile

Reprinted by permission of Off the Mark and Mark Parisi. ©1997 Mark Parisi.

The Hill

Some choices we live not only once but a thousand times over, remembering them for the rest of our lives.

Richard Bach

As my eight-year-old feet pumped the pedals, stones spit out behind the rear tire to form what I imagined to be motorcycle exhaust. When I neared the end of the drive where the gravel met asphalt, I slammed the right pedal backward, making the back tire slide sideways and my bike come to a skidding stop.

As I put down my left foot and leaned the bicycle toward the driveway, I saw my friend Timmy running to catch up. He beamed with almost as much pride as I felt after my first successful sideways stop. After all, Timmy taught me on his bike how to ride when other kids made fun of the fact that I did not know how to ride, much less own a bicycle. He was easy to understand, encouraging and patient; he was the perfect coach.

Timmy's grin faded as he got closer and peered over my shoulder. I heard the sound of a boot kicking gravel off the asphalt back onto the driveway. A stray rock made a slight "ping" sound as it struck one of the spokes.

It was my dad.

As he scooted the last piece of gravel back into the driveway where it belonged, he raised his eyes to glare at me. He always seemed to want me to be perfect, but it seemed I couldn't please him. My bedroom wasn't clean enough; I couldn't get to the dinner table fast enough; my toys weren't cared for enough. He moved in front of the bicycle, straddled the front tire, and leaned over the handlebars until he was directly in front of me.

He looked briefly at Timmy, and then turned back to me.

"I thought if I let you and Timmy ride the bike, you agreed to keep it in the driveway?"

"But, Dad, we didn't get in the road," I replied.

"You were close enough!" he stormed.

"I had it under control," I defended.

"Under control? If you had slid one more foot, you would have been in the street. What if a car had been coming?"

"But, there wasn't, Dad. I looked. . . ."

He cut me off. "You just don't know how dangerous

this hill is, do you? Tall bushes line the street, and then the road curves at the bottom of our hill and then climbs another hill bigger than ours. If you get on the road, a driver wouldn't even see you comin'!"

I pulled my right leg over the bar of the bicycle and looked at Timmy. "You might as well take this, Timmy. I'm never allowed to do anything."

My father looked at me sternly as he surrendered the bike to Timmy. Timmy gave me an understanding look as he walked his bike to the "dangerous" road, put his left foot on the left pedal, and pushed the bicycle forward using his right foot to start the bike in motion.

"See, Dad, Timmy is allowed to ride on the street."

"Timmy isn't my son, Sherm. The only reason I haven't bought you a bike or even taught you to ride is because of this dangerous hill. Besides, Timmy lives on the flat area above the hill and has plenty of safe road to ride on near his home."

I trudged toward our house with my dad trailing behind me.

I didn't get to ride the bike again until two weeks later. It was a perfect afternoon in early June with blue skies. My mom was lying on the couch with a headache, and my dad was fishing. Timmy and I used that chance to ride his bicycle.

We were having a great time taking turns riding on the gravel driveway, hopping over the hump in the middle of the drive. With Timmy's encouragement, I dared for the first time to ride with no hands. It felt good to be doing something that my dad wouldn't like without him breathing down my neck. I felt free to have a great time for once.

Timmy slyly looked at me before speaking, "Hey, Sherm, why don't we try going down the hill?"

Riding on the driveway without permission was one thing, but riding down the hill was another. I thought about doing it for a minute, but I was very clear that riding down the hill was forbidden.

Finally, I agreed to be Timmy's lookout. I stood at the top of the hill and watched for cars coming down the other hill. If it were safe, I would yell, "Clear!" to Timmy.

The first time he did it was so exciting. He pedaled hard for about fifty feet to get his speed up, and then he coasted the rest of way. I could see him until he turned the curve and started up the other hill. He disappeared around the tall bushes and then came out to where I saw him slow up and turn around to come back. It went perfectly.

Timmy yelled as he walked his bike back up our steep hill. "It was unbelievable, Sherm. You *have* to try it!"

My mom was asleep; my dad was away. There was no one to stop or scold me. I decided I had to take the chance.

Timmy watched to see if the hill was free of oncoming traffic. Before I went for it, I felt a twist in my stomach. It was a feeling I hadn't felt before. I was going to try something that was forbidden. But I felt great. I felt daring. I felt free.

When Timmy shouted that it was okay to go, I started down the hill. The wind began to blow into my ears as the speed began to rise. The bike seemed to control itself as I sped down the hill.

I thought I heard Timmy yelling from behind me, but I figured he was just excited and enjoying my ride as much as I was. But when I cleared the curve, the screeching tires not only alerted my ears, but also opened my eyes to what was happening. For the first time in my life, I could actually hear my own heart-beat as I slammed the bike's brakes.

Somehow, the car stopped before the bicycle's front tire hit the front bumper. As the back wheel began to lift off the ground, I began to tumble over the handle-bars. I clearly saw the hood of the car rush toward my face, and then the windshield wipers, and finally the windshield as I slid headfirst until I was face to face with the person behind the steering wheel. I immediately recognized the wide-open eyes staring through the windshield because they belonged to my father!

I hadn't been scared until that moment, but I felt a tremble start in my toes and run like a wave through my legs, then my torso, and finally end in a huge shudder at my head.

Dad jumped out of the car and quickly came to my rescue. Without saying a word, he checked me for broken bones. His hands went over my legs and then my arms as he asked me where I hurt. After realizing that I was bruised but all right, he rolled me over to my back, gently lifted me off the hood of the car, and sat me on my feet. He left the car parked in the middle of the street and walked me to our house. Timmy came running toward us, and Dad surprised me when his voice quivered slightly as he softly asked Timmy to grab his bike and go home.

I got to the back door first, but Dad reached over me and opened the door. He nudged me forward to go on in. I stayed ahead of him until we got to the living room. My mother stirred and began to rise up from her nap.

I had been spanked with an open hand across the bottom when I had been young and did something dumb, but this time I had been older and bolder. I figured I'd get more than just a lecture this time.

But instead of another lecture, my dad struggled through tears to say, "Son, I could have lost you. I could have lost you. Nothing would be worse. Nothing."

The next day was Sunday. I remember being at church and hoping that God was listening to my prayer of thanks that nothing worse had happened to me or to my father. When we got home, my dad didn't even take off his church clothes. He went straight for the shed and then straight to the bushes by the street. He didn't stop chopping until they all fell to the ground in a heap.

When he was finished, I walked over to be next to him. I finally realized that my dad, who I always thought was an uncaring and sometimes mean man, was actually a caring, loving father after all.

Sherm Perkins

A Little Birdie . . . a Big Responsibility

I've always loved animals—cats, dogs, fish—you name it. My dad also loved animals and taught me how to take care of them. That was one of the first main responsibilities I ever had, and I was proud of it. I felt so confident that I thought I could take care of any animal. But, as the saying goes, "Be careful what you wish for."

When I was about nine years old, I went to Marine World with some friends. The day was beautiful and went by quickly. As we were passing through the main gates to leave, I saw a small crowd of kids who were probably a few years older than me. They were surrounding something on the sidewalk. Curious, I went up to the crowd and saw that they were staring at a small baby bird. It was so small it could fit in the palm of a hand. It didn't have any feathers and was bright pink. I probably would have walked away, but I saw the bird move. It was still alive, and no one was helping it.

Shocked, I pushed my way through the crowd, picked up the baby bird, and held it close to my chest. By this time, the older kids were bored and left me alone with my new find. As I stared at the little creature, I was shocked to see that it had been hurt. There was a burn mark on its stomach, and as I looked around, I quickly saw a cigarette butt that had been stepped on. Clearly, some horrible person had taken the cigarette and used it on this poor, helpless animal. I was so angry I almost cried, but instead I decided I would take care of the baby bird.

I took the bird home and didn't tell my parents because I was afraid they would make me get rid of it. Taking care of a bird was different from taking care of a dog or cat, so I needed to find out for myself how to nurse the bird back to health.

I named the bird Tweety, after the Looney Tunes character. I put Tweety in a small shoe box with plenty of tissue paper to keep him warm. When I went to school the next day, I snuck the box into my classroom and hoped the teacher wouldn't find it, but she did. I told her I couldn't leave Tweety at home alone and begged her to let me keep the box in the classroom. She agreed, as long as Tweety didn't become a distraction. And I had to promise not to bring him to school again.

Taking care of Tweety was harder than I thought. The only thing I knew about birds was that the mother bird caught worms, chewed them up, and then spit them out to feed the babies. There was no way I was going to do that, so I gave Tweety small droplets of milk from a straw. I caught a fly and tried to feed it to him, but Tweety couldn't open his mouth wide enough. I was frustrated but still confident that I was doing the right thing.

As the days went by, I left Tweety in his box in my room while I was at school. I put dead flies in his box, hoping he would eat them, and I continued to give him milk when I got home. I really thought I was helping.

On the fourth day of taking care of Tweety, I came home from school to find Tweety motionless and not breathing. As much as I didn't want to believe it, Tweety was dead. I had never experienced an animal dying before, especially one that I had been taking caring of. I felt like I had failed, and it was my fault. I fell to the floor and began crying.

My dad came into my room when he heard all the noise. I was so upset that I could barely get the words out to tell him what had happened. I still hadn't told my parents about Tweety, so I cried even harder, thinking I was going to get into trouble.

My dad sat down next to me on the floor and held me tight. When I had calmed down some, he asked me where I had found Tweety. I told him the whole story.

"You took care of this bird all by yourself?" he asked me.

I nodded. "But it didn't even matter because he's

dead!" I sobbed. "I'm never going to take care of an animal again!" My dad knew that I loved animals too much to really mean that.

"Look at it this way. If you hadn't found Tweety, someone could have done something even worse to him, and he wouldn't have lived past one day. Because you cared and took responsibility for him, he lived longer than he should have," my dad explained to me.

I hadn't really thought about it that way before.

Then he said to me, "If you focus on the negative instead of the positive, you will become a negative person."

"So what I did was a good thing, even though Tweety died?" I asked my dad.

"Of course," he answered.

After we buried Tweety in the backyard, my dad explained to me that while I was right in saving Tweety, I didn't think about the huge responsibility I had taken upon myself. Being responsible was a good thing, but not asking for help when the situation got out of hand was a mistake.

Now that I'm older and my responsibilities have gotten bigger, I still carry my dad's advice with me. While I haven't taken care of another bird, I've continued taking care of cats, dogs, and fish. That's all the responsibility I need.

Dania Denise Mallette

Munchy

Never neglect the little things. Never skimp on that extra effort, that additional few minutes . . . that delivery of the very best that you can do.

Og Mandino

It was bedtime for me and my new hamster, Munchy, so I picked him up, walked to my nanny's room and shut the gate on his cage . . . or so I thought. I gave my nanny and my parents good-night kisses, and then went to my room, laid my head on the pillow, and fell into a deep sleep.

The next day at school, I couldn't wait to tell my friends about my new pet hamster. I bragged about the little ball of orange and white fur that was waiting for me at home. I told the same story of how I had named him Munchy because of the funny and cute way he munched on his food. "He's the cutest thing!

He's so small!" I told everyone who would listen. I bragged and bragged like a CD player stuck on repeat.

My best friend, Melanie, and I made plans for her to come over soon to play with him. Finally, three o'clock came around, and it was time for my dad to pick me up and drop me off at home. I was so excited to see my favorite new friend again.

"Hi, Mami. Hi, Eva," I said as I walked in and put my stuff on the kitchen table. But my mother and nanny, Eva, just stared back at me. They looked like they were about to ride a roller coaster—like they were nervous, but wanted to pretend they were excited, so they painted on a smile.

"Was Munchy good today?" I asked them, guessing that something wasn't right.

"Well, we wanted to talk to you about that," my mom responded.

"Uh-oh, what happened?" I asked, sort of afraid of hearing the answer.

"Last night, Eva felt something crawl up her bed and around her neck. She picked it up and threw it across the room without thinking. And Munchy is not in his cage. Are you sure you closed it last night?"

"Ummm . . . yes?" I answered with a question.

"Well, it seems that you didn't close the cage properly because Munchy is missing. That wasn't very responsible of you. You'll need to learn to be more responsible if you're going to take care of Munchy. We don't know if he got hurt when Eva threw him. We've looked and looked all day and haven't found him anywhere."

I stood there feeling very worried and guilty.

"Now you know why it's important to make sure you do what we ask and listen to us, right?"

"Yes, Mami," I said.

"Okay. Now why don't you go look for him? Maybe you'll have more luck than us."

I looked and looked the rest of the day and never found him. I looked in my room, Eva's room, the bathroom, the kitchen, upstairs and downstairs, but I saw no sign of him. We didn't find him the next day either. I felt terrible because I knew it was my fault. From the day that Munchy went missing, I promised myself that I would always try to be as careful and responsible as I could.

One day, I came home from school, and my mom was getting ready to vacuum. She went into the closet, opened the door, and guess who was staring up at her? A cute little orange and white ball of fur, that's who. Munchy was alive and perfectly unharmed! I was so happy to see my friend again and to know that he was okay.

From then on, I made sure that the cage door was always closed before I put him away, and Munchy has never been lost again.

Lloret Pelayo

4

MAKING GOOD CHOICES

We all have choices, you and I.
One is to laugh, and one is to cry.
One is to be wrong, one is to be right.
One is to be peaceable, one is to fight.
One is to love, one is to hate.
One is to be early, one is to be late.
One is to be truthful, one is to lie.
One is to fail, one is to try.
One is to quit, or to follow things through.
The final choice is up to you.

Dontay Hall

Starting Over

All you need is trust and a little bit of pixie dust.

Peter Pan

"Oops!"

My piggy bank slipped from my hands and fell, breaking into pieces. The coins scattered all over the room. I quickly ran to pick them all up as my grandfather gazed at me.

The piggy bank had been a gift from him. It had an opening through which one could put money in, but it was not big enough to reach in and get the money out. "That's the whole idea," he explained. "The bank will help you save your money so that, at the end of the year, you might have enough for that bicycle you want."

Whenever he gave me a little bit of money, which was often, he would say, "This is for spending. But you can save some and put it in the piggy bank if you want to save it up." Whenever he gave me larger amounts, it was clearly for saving in the piggy bank.

For some time, this worked fine. I loved shaking the piggy bank and hearing the clinking sound of the coins. As it became heavier, I grew more and more excited, dreaming about what I could do with my savings.

Until . . .

One day, my friends and I wanted to visit the new ice-cream shop in town. Even after pooling everybody's money together, we did not have enough for each of us to get an ice cream.

"Why don't you take some out of your piggy bank?" my friend asked.

"No. I can't," I replied firmly. "There is a slit for putting the money in, but no way for taking any out. Besides, my grandfather told me that I need to save the money until the end of the year."

"Come on. Show me the piggy bank. I'll show you how you can take out the money," said my friend, the know-it-all.

I didn't want to, but I felt pressured by my friends. We took the piggy bank to the park and tried our best to shake out the money.

I must confess that it was fun. Someone got a quarter, another one got a dollar bill, and one managed to pull out a five-dollar bill.

Finally, we managed to get enough money to buy everyone an ice cream.

From then on, I became an expert at taking money

out of my piggy bank. Soon, it became a habit, and I started taking out money whenever I wanted it, without a second thought.

I was doing just that when Grandpa walked in.

It was then that I panicked and dropped the piggy bank. It broke.

As I picked up the last coin, it was painfully clear that I had spent most of the money in it.

I burst into tears, and Grandpa came over and hugged me, not saying a single word. He let me cry as much as I wanted. I did not know what to say.

The rest of the day, I kept thinking how irresponsible I had been. Would Grandpa ever trust me again?

Soon, I got the answer.

The next day, he presented me with another piggy bank, identical to the one that had broken.

"Let's try starting over," said Grandpa, and then he kissed me on my forehead. He pulled out five dollars and gave it to me. "I know this bank will most likely have a much longer life," he said. I think he knew I had learned my lesson.

Blushing, I put the five-dollar bill inside.

Jamuna Rangachari

Friends Forever

If you live to be 100, I hope I live to be 100 minus one day, so I never have to live without you.

Winnie-the-Pooh

"Hey, Jenna, do you think we'll still be friends when we're eighty-two?" I stopped bouncing on the trampoline when I saw a puzzled look on my friend's face. Boy, did her look say it all! It was clear she was wondering where in the world I had come up with such a random question. Being such good friends, it had become easy to read each other's minds. So, while I waited for Jenna to answer, I started wondering what life would be like without her.

Definitely not the same, that's for sure! Losing Jenna would be like losing a very close sister. We hang out together as often as we can. We laugh together. We cry together. We give each other advice. We even look a little bit alike. When I spend the night at her house, I feel like part of Jenna's family. If it weren't for Jenna, I don't know where in my life's journey I would be, but I'm sure it wouldn't be here.

Suddenly, my thoughts were interrupted. "Of course, we'll still be friends when we're eighty-two," Jenna announced loudly. I gave Jenna a friendly stare, and she returned it. We stared at each other until we were laughing so hard that tears were streaming down my face. That moment was one of the most important in our friendship together and, as you might have guessed, eighty-two was our new magic number. But that's not where the story ends.

The next year, in fourth grade, we met Jamie. Jamie had just moved from California, and since she lived in the same neighborhood as Jenna and me, the three of us soon clicked into a really tight group of friends. We played together almost every day. We shared our biggest secrets and crushes, and even came up with crazy ideas to make a little extra cash for the summer. I was happy to have reached out to Jamie as well as getting even closer to my other good friends. Things couldn't have been better, and I thought even time couldn't pull us apart, but that is where I was sadly mistaken.

The three of us started fighting a lot—and not just small fights where your friend won't return a CD you let her borrow. No, these fights involved hurt feelings, crying, taking sides, nasty e-mails, and mean glares. Before Christmas, we had a really big fight, and it was just my luck that Jamie and Jenna were ganging up on me, both saying I was bossy and couldn't keep my mouth closed. I felt helpless and alone. They wouldn't even talk to me at school unless they had some mean insult for me. I had very little hope for the future, and I was almost positive that Christmas, my birthday, and New Year's Day would be horrible! *Why is this happening to me?* I thought. *How can I not even know what I did and have things end up this bad?*

That's why I was surprised when Jenna came to my house and gave me an awesome Christmas card she had made for me. I was so sure that she was still disappointed with me, and now I was getting a really nice card that she even made herself. *Is time going to prove me wrong once again?*

"Wow," I said, breaking the silence as we stood on either side of my front door. "Thanks."

"Okay . . . well . . . I have to go," she said softly.

"Okay. See you later then. . . ." and I closed the door and headed back to my mom's bedroom to finish watching a movie.

"Who was that at the door?" my mom asked.

"It was Jenna," I explained, showing her the card. I pressed play on the VCR, but I wasn't watching the TV screen. Instead, I was admiring the front of the card, which was decorated with snowmen, snowflakes, and a perfect image of Santa Claus. After a few minutes of admiring the front, I decided to peek inside.

The card started off with "Merry Christmas" (what else would you put in a Christmas card?), but then, farther down the page, it said, "I am so glad we're friends. I am sorry about what I said when we were fighting. A fight won't stop us from being friends. Besides, we said we were going to be friends even when we're eighty-two."

I stopped reading and started laughing. I couldn't believe I had forgotten what she said that day in her back yard. I couldn't believe I had been so selfish in trying to get even and making my friends feel sorry for me that I had forgotten about real friendship.

Instead of drifting farther and farther apart, and eventually going our separate ways, like my friendship with Jamie, Jenna and I held strong, even through the bad times. Jenna ended up being my true friend. Isn't that what a true friend is? Someone who chooses to stick with you every day of your life, even when you're eighty-two.

Darian Smith

Max and the Purple BMX Mongoose Bike

Honesty is the best policy.

Miguel de Cervantes

I sat next to my sleeping, two-year-old, baby sister in the middle seat of our parents' van. Mom had insisted that I go with her to pick up Dad from work while his car was in the shop. Across from Dad's office is a store called Sunshine Bikes. That was the day my eleven-year-old eyes first saw the purple BMX Mongoose bike.

From that day on, just about all I could think about was that purple BMX Mongoose bike. I even drew pictures of the bike instead of paying attention in class.

Every evening afterward, at five-thirty, I eagerly went along with Mom and my baby sister to get Dad. And every day I let it be known, "I love that bike!" or

"I want that bike!" or "I've got to have that bike!"

Mom usually answered, "That's nice, dear."

But Dad's reply was, "Max, you have a perfectly good bike in the garage."

"My bike is old and ugly," I'd argue.

The next Sunday at church, the sermon was about prayer. I only half-listened until the reverend said, "Through prayer, with God's help, all things are possible."

Including getting a bike my parents don't think I need? I wondered.

When church ended, the congregation shook hands with the minister. As I reached out my hand, I asked, "Is there any limit to what you should bother God with?"

Reverend Lindsey said, "You can talk to God about anything. Nothing is too great or too unimportant to share with God."

When I got home, I hurried upstairs and through the door with the sign reading PRIVATE in big orange letters. I crossed the green carpeted floor and flopped down on my bed to have a long talk with God.

I told God about the purple BMX Mongoose bike. "I want that bike so bad. I'm sure my happiness depends on it. If you just get me that bike, I will never do anything bad again."

A few days later, the bike was no longer in the window. "Where is my bike?" I shouted.

"At home in the garage," Mom replied.

"Not *that* bike!" I explained. "The one in the bike-store window."

"Maybe they sold it," Mom said.

"I wanted that bike," I whined.

"I'm sorry, Max," Mom said.

"There are other bikes," Dad said.

Miserable, I knew I'd never be happy again. Maybe God didn't hear my prayer.

About a week later, coming home from school, I tripped over something. Lying in the weeds, near some wooded lots, was a bike—the *exact* bike from the store.

"Hey, whose bike is this?" I shouted, scanning the area.

No one replied, and there was no one in sight. *Maybe the bike is here for me, the answer to my prayer. I can't leave the bike of my dreams lying in the weeds.* So I took it home.

I hid the bike behind the garage next to our house. *Just until I tell Mom and Dad,* I thought.

Every day after school, I sat behind the garage admiring the purple BMX Mongoose bike. I didn't feel like riding and didn't feel as happy as I thought I would. Thinking about the bike now made my stomach tighten up and feel uncomfortable.

A few days later, at school during lunch, someone said, "Did you hear about Tyler Weston, in the other fifth-grade class? He lost the new BMX Mongoose bike he just got for his birthday. He left it by the stream while he was playing in the woods. It got dark, and he couldn't find it."

"I'd never go off and leave a new bike like that. He

doesn't deserve to have that bike," I said to Paul, my best friend.

"Kids say he's nice. In fact, the next day after school, everyone helped him search for his bike, but they couldn't find it. I heard Tyler's upset because his dad worked overtime to buy the bike for Tyler's birthday," said Paul.

For the rest of the day, I couldn't stop thinking about Tyler Weston.

After school, I went to my room. My stomach ached. I sat at my desk, staring at a drawing of the bike. *There must be a way to fix this*, I thought. Then I remembered how the reverend had said that through prayer, with God's help, all things are possible.

"Lord, help me know right from wrong. If I do make the wrong choice, show me the way to correct what I have done wrong."

Mom came to my door. "Max, I didn't see you when you came home. Are you all right?" Picking up the drawing, Mom asked, "Are you still upset about the bike?"

"Kind of . . ." I told her everything, including about praying for the bike. "I need to return the bike to Tyler."

Mom put her arms around me. "Mrs. Weston is in my Tuesday evening women's group. We met at her home last week. They live in a red-brick home about seven blocks from here. You get the bike. I'll get your baby sister."

At Tyler's house, I told Tyler and his parents about finding the bike.

Tyler's father hugged me and said, "Thank you. We prayed someone would find the bike and return it. You've answered our prayer."

Riding home, I smiled, thinking about how thankful Tyler and his parents were. My stomach began to feel better. "Mom . . . I thought I needed the bike to be happy, and that getting the bike was the answer to my prayer. But I feel happy because Tyler and his parents were happy to get the bike back. And I am proud of myself for doing the right thing."

Mom drove on in silence, but her smile told me she was proud of me, too.

Max Sampsell as told to Joi Sampsell

Being True to Myself

Between two evils, choose neither; between two goods, choose both.

Tryon Edwards

My parents and I had been planning my brother's birthday party since the beginning of March. Johnny would be six years old in two days. My mom was going to bake her special chocolate cake with white icing. As I watched her, I thought, *Gee, I wonder what I can do to make my brother's birthday special.*

I decided to empty my coin jar and see how much money I had saved. I was disappointed to find much less than I had imagined. "Oh, no, I only have about three dollars," I muttered to myself. I knew my parents had already bought a present for me to give to Johnny, but I wanted to buy him something I had chosen myself and with the money I had saved. I wanted to buy him the paint-by-number kit I had seen at the store, but the set cost more than I had saved.

Disappointed, I went into my parents' bedroom where my dad kept loose change on top of the dresser. I stood on my tiptoes and saw some dimes, nickels, and a few quarters. I carefully counted out what I needed to make up the difference. *I'm sure Dad won't mind just this once,* I thought. However, I was soon overcome by guilt. Even though there was no one else in the bedroom, I felt like I was being watched. Mom was always telling us about the importance of honesty. She had even made up a short poem for us:

> *Always be honest in everything you say and do,*
> *Because God is always watching over you.*
> *When there seems to be no one else around,*
> *That's where God is always found.*

Maybe my plan wasn't such a great idea after all, I thought. My dad would be home in another hour, and my mom was busy in the kitchen preparing dinner. I jingled the change around in my pocket while wondering what to do.

I grabbed my jacket from the closet and headed toward the door.

"Where are you going, honey?" Mom asked.

"Oh, just up to the corner store," I replied.

"Well, don't stay out too long. Daddy will be home soon."

"Okay, Mom."

Once I got to the store, I took the paint-by-number kit from the shelf.

"Can I help you, young lady?" the salesclerk asked.

"No . . . I'm just looking, thank you," I said.

"That's a really nice paint kit. We sell a lot of them and, as you can see, that's the last one," she said.

I nodded my head in agreement, but finally decided to do what was right.

I placed the paint-by-number kit back on the shelf and headed home.

Luckily, once I got home, Mom was busy talking on the phone, so I was able to slip past the kitchen without being noticed. I went to my parents' room to return the coins I had taken. I arranged them into a neat stack—just like they were before—and sighed with relief, knowing I had done the right thing.

I knew the paint kit would have been the perfect present for my brother. I would just have to wait until I saved the extra money I needed. I figured I could earn it by doing odd jobs around the house. Mrs. Davis, the salesclerk, had even agreed that she would hold the paint set behind the counter for me until I had enough money to pay for it.

I wasn't able to buy the paint kit until two weeks later, but it seemed extra special when I was finally able to lay *my* money on the counter. I smiled as I raced home knowing I had made the right decision.

Terri Meehan

Is Sixteen Enough?

You never find yourself until you face the truth.

Pearl Bailey

When I was in first grade, parents were required to buy certain school supplies. Crayons were on the list. Because my parents had five children to buy supplies for, they bought me the box with only eight crayons.

I was proud enough of my box of crayons until I got to school and saw that just about everyone else who sat near me in class had the big box of sixty-four crayons.

This isn't fair! Why do I have so few crayons, and they have so many? I thought. So, I told my parents that my box of crayons was stolen.

Like I'd hoped, my parents bought another box of crayons for me. It wasn't, however, the box of sixty-four brilliant colors I wanted so badly. It was another box of eight.

I placed my new crayons in my pencil box along with the original eight. Sixteen was better than eight, but was sixteen crayons enough? Again, that evening, I told my parents the same story: someone had stolen my crayons. Again, I had a brand-new box the next day. It was another box of eight! I now had twenty-four crayons; three of each color, but not sixty-four *different* colors.

Foolishly, I decided to try one more time for a box of sixty-four. This time, I told my parents that the teacher said I had to have the larger box. As soon as I told them this, I knew my father was on to me by the way he looked at me.

"Who do you think is stealing your crayons each day? Why aren't they stealing anyone else's crayons?" he asked.

Shrugging my shoulders, I answered, "I don't know."

"Well," my father said, "I think I should come to school with you tomorrow to talk with your teacher and see what we can do about this situation."

Oh, no! If he did that, he'd know I had been lying. My friends would know, and especially my teacher would know. I squirmed and shuffled my feet. How could I keep this from happening?

"Of course," said my father, "if your crayons are just misplaced instead of stolen . . . and you were to find them, I guess there'd be no need for me to come."

Miraculously, all my crayons showed up the next day. After school, my father asked me, "Did you find them?"

"Yes," I answered, trying to act like I was amazed.

"That's wonderful," my father said, as he gave me a hug.

Looking back, I can see the wisdom in my father's simple solution to this problem. He knew that I knew that he knew, and he gave me a way out.

Perhaps, after that incident, if I had lied again, he wouldn't have given me an "out," but I made sure from then on that he would never have to do that again.

Christine M. Smith

Disney Magic

When I was about six years old, my family and I went to Disneyland one weekend and had a wonderful day full of excitement. Little did I know that the real excitement wasn't to begin until that night.

While we watched the fireworks, I began to get an urge to go to the restroom, but I didn't want to miss the show. I overheard my sister Isabel talking to my mom, and I got closer to them to hear what they were talking about.

"Mom, I'm going to the bathroom with Lizette, okay?" said Isabel.

"Okay," my mom replied, "but stay together. I don't want any of you getting lost."

The second I saw my sisters leaving, I didn't think twice before running after them—without telling my parents. As I followed them through the huge crowd of people, I started to lose sight of them. I began to panic as I scanned the crowd for them. Crazy thoughts ran through my head like, *What if I never see my family again?*

I gave up trying to find my sisters and tried to get back to my family, but I was completely mixed up. After searching for what seemed like forever, I couldn't hold back my tears, and I started crying like I had never cried before.

"Mommy!" I cried out. But everyone around me was too caught up by the fireworks to pay any attention to me.

I tried to stop the scary thoughts that were going through my head and started running as fast as I could . . . anywhere . . . everywhere. I was going crazy. *I'm only six, and I've gotten lost. What have I done? How could I have been so dumb to run off without telling anyone?* I thought.

With my face wet from tears, I kept running, pulling at people's pants and crying, "Mommy!" I was hoping, *wishing,* that one of these adults would be one of my parents.

Luckily, I tugged at a lady who worked at Disneyland, and she asked me, "Are you lost?"

"Yeeesss!" I cried.

She picked me up and carried me through the crowd as she kept asking me where my parents had been standing. As I began to feel safe in the lady's arms, I calmed down and thought for a few minutes. I remembered we had been leaning against a wooden fence.

She carried me around the wooden fence, asking random people, "Is this your child?"

"No. Sorry," everyone kept saying.

You're sorry? Look at me. I'm looking for my mommy, I thought.

Finally, through the crowd of people, I recognized a face. I was so happy. "Mommy!" I shouted as I pointed toward her so the lady could carry me to her. When the lady put me down, I ran to my mom and gave her a huge hug. I couldn't let go of her. I didn't want to lose her again. As I cried in my mother's arms, my family thanked the nice lady for everything she had done for me.

For the rest of the evening and the entire next day, I was more concerned with making sure that my parents were within my sight at all times than I was with seeing the sights at Disneyland.

I look back at these memories and laugh at myself, but to this day, I always make sure to tell someone where I am going before I run off.

Bryan Martinez

Courage on the Court

Andy has a lot of courage. He's never wrestled a bear. He's never hiked ten miles in a blizzard or saved a cat stuck in a tree. Not yet. But he has stood up to something scarier—the guys on his basketball team. And that was when he was only ten years old.

Last season, Andy's basketball team, the Blues, came from behind in an amazing finals play-off. You know who the coach was? A high-school player.

As the season went along, Andy's team had lost more games than they had won and were in sixth place out of eight teams. In the finals, they had to go against the tough, third-ranked Green team. But the Blues were hungry for a win when they played the first round of finals. They started out scoring the first basket and wouldn't let the Green team catch up. That was their game plan. Squash and score, and it worked. Andy's team outscored the Green team by twelve points, and they went through to round two.

Their next game in the finals was the following

Saturday. Andy's pretty tall, so he always did the tip-off. But the Yellow team guy he faced was as tall as Andy's dad—without even jumping. He just stood there with his arm raised like he was answering a question in math class and tapped the ball to another Yellow guy who took it down the court and scored.

It went downhill from there. None of the guys on the Blue team could make their baskets. It was as if the rims were smeared with grease. The Blue team lost by nine points, but it wasn't over yet. They were still able to play another team that had lost. They were still able to take third place and a trophy.

The next Saturday, Andy and the rest of the Blue team got to the gym extra early. They were playing the Red team, and Andy knew a lot of those guys from being on their teams from other seasons. He even had the coach of that team two years before.

The gym was so quiet at tip-off that Andy heard the kid facing him breathe. The ref blasted her whistle. Andy's fingers scuffed the ball, but the Red player managed to knock it to his Red teammate.

The numbers on the scoreboard jumped back and forth just like the basketball. Andy managed to make a couple of baskets. Even though he wore his lucky basketball shorts, Blue had slipped behind by one.

Fifteen seconds were left, and the Blue team had the ball. They could still win. Suddenly, the ball was out of bounds.

"Blue ball," the ref said. "I didn't see who touched it last."

As a Blue player hopped over the line at center court to throw in the ball, Andy later said it was one of those moments that lasted only a second, but felt like forever. The ref hadn't seen who had touched it last, but Andy had.

Andy, like the rest of his teammates, wanted to win—badly. If Blue got the ball and made a basket, they would win by one point. And they had time, *if* Andy kept quiet.

"Ref, it hit my foot," Andy confessed.

"Thank you," the ref said as she took the ball back from Blue and handed it to Red. There was some major groaning from the Blues.

Although it was close, the Blue team lost by three points, but the boys still wound up with shiny, fourth-place medals on red, white, and blue ribbons. Everyone thought that was cool.

Andy's old coach from the Red team came over to him before he left the gym.

"Andy, what you did in there," he nodded toward the court, "made me proud of you. And I'm not talking about your playing. You know what I mean?"

When Andy was asked if he had been afraid of what his teammates would say when he confessed, he shrugged. "They were mad, but I knew they wouldn't hate me. But if I didn't say anything, I knew *I* would hate me for a long time afterward."

Sandy Green

Grandpa's Pig

If you could kick the person in the pants responsible for most of your trouble, you wouldn't sit for a month.

Theodore Roosevelt

When I was a little girl, I loved visiting my grandparents at their ranch. I enjoyed helping Grandma pick huge zucchini, cucumbers, string beans, and giant pumpkins in Grandpa's garden. In the summer, I filled buckets with fruit from the orchard. But, of all my chores, the one I loved the most was feeding Nettie, Grandpa's enormous pet pig.

Nettie's soft brown eyes would twinkle at me from inside her big mud pen. Her pointed ears would be perked at attention while her snout twitched hungrily for more food.

But Grandpa would simply say, "No more food for you, Nettie ol' girl. You've had enough today."

"She'll eat me out of house and home if I let her," Grandpa would say each time we fed Nettie. "She just doesn't know when to stop."

I loved giving Nettie her favorite treats. "Couldn't I please give her just a few more prickly pears?" I pleaded. But Grandpa's answer was always, "No."

Even though Grandpa warned me not to overfeed Nettie, I often brought her bags of freshly picked and peeled prickly pears. Nettie adored the sweet treats and could never get enough of them. I poked the pears through the open slats of her wooden pen because Grandpa always warned me to keep out of Nettie's pen.

One day, after I heard Grandpa's truck rumble off for town, I picked a bag of Nettie's favorite prickly pears, carried them to her pen, and tugged at the gate. But Grandpa had closed the gate securely before leaving that day, and the latch was too high up for me to reach. So I climbed up the rough, splintered planks and, using one of Grandpa's long garden rakes, managed to pull open the gate. Below me, Grandpa's huge pig thrashed in her pen. Suddenly, I lost my footing and toppled down into Nettie's muddy pen, landing on her broad shoulders. Startled, she raised a powerful hind leg and crashed open the gate. A moment later, she was running around the farmyard. Terrified as I held tightly to Nettie's ears, the huge pig took me on a painfully bumpy ride.

Nettie squealed loudly as she kicked up dust and trampled over anything that got in her path. She trotted over Grandma's flower beds and plowed through her freshly hung wash, scattering clean white laundry all over the farmyard. I took a wild piggyback ride through Grandpa's vegetable garden, mashing his prize-winning tomatoes and cantaloupes.

Then, suddenly, without warning, the huge pig stopped. I slid off her back head-over-heels, like an out-of-control skyrocket.

When I landed, it was right in the middle of Grandpa's thorny prickly pear patch. I let out a yell that echoed through the valley. Nettie just couldn't resist her favorite treats. After stopping to enjoy several nibbles, the giant pig whirled around, kicked up a cloud of dust, and went running down the road and over a hill until she finally disappeared from sight.

Grandma, hearing my loud cries for help, came running out from the ranch house. Finding me in the middle of the prickly pear patch and seeing her garden in a mess, she quickly figured out what had happened. Grandma sighed, "What's your grandpa going to say when he returns home and sees this, and finds his pig gone?"

I didn't have an answer, but we couldn't think about that now. We had more important matters to attend to, like removing all those painful thorns from my rear end.

After Grandma had pulled out the last thorn, she sent me to bed to rest and wait for Grandpa to return. I just couldn't stand the thought of seeing Grandpa's face when he came home and found his precious old

Nettie gone and his farmyard a wreck.

Late that afternoon, the skies began to darken, and the wind howled through the trees. The local radio station reported that a windstorm was coming to the area. Within minutes, wind howled through the valley. It scattered leaves and blew open corral gates, setting animals free for miles around.

When Grandpa finally arrived home later that evening, to my great joy, riding in the back of his truck was old Nettie, just as happy as a pig could be, munching on prickly pears.

"That sure was some freak weather we had while I was gone," Grandpa declared. "All the nearby ranches are cluttered with trash, and folks are chasing after their animals for miles around. Lucky for me, I found old Nettie just down the road nibbling on a prickly pear tree."

Grandpa figured that the messy farmyard and Nettie getting out was because of the windstorm. But Grandma knew the truth. I held my breath, waiting for her to blow the whistle on me, but to my relief, Grandma felt I'd been punished enough by those painful prickly pear thorns. She never told Grandpa a word about my wild piggyback ride.

For weeks afterward, I couldn't sit down without a cushion beneath me. And for years after that, just the thought of that prickly pear patch gave me good reason to think twice before I ever disobeyed anyone ever again.

Cookie Curci

"I warned him about putting bullfrogs in his pockets."

5

MAKING AND ACCEPTING CHANGES

Life belongs to the living, and he who lives must be prepared for changes.

Johann Wolfgang von Goethe

Still Loved

You cannot change the circumstances, the seasons, or the wind, but you can change yourself. That is something you have charge of.

Jim Rohn

When I was about ten years old, my parents got in a huge argument that changed my life forever. Every time before that, they would always make up, but this time I had a feeling it was going to be different. This time, my parents didn't talk to each other for days, and my dad slept on our pullout couch down in the basement.

Then we went to the county fair as a family. My mom and dad started talking and having fun together again, so I thought everything was okay.

I asked my mom, "You and Daddy are getting along a lot better, aren't you?"

"Well, I don't know about that," she answered.

I was so confused. I think my brother was, too, but he was just a normal thirteen-year-old and wasn't brave enough to admit how he was feeling.

Then the night came when my parents called my brother and me to come into the living room. They asked us to sit on the couch because they had to talk to us about something.

My dad began by saying, "Cameron, Karissa, your mom and I just can't seem to get along together any longer. We have worked on it and worked on it. We decided it would be best for me to move out and see if that helps."

"No, Daddy!" I yelled. "You can't leave us!" My brother began yelling and screaming, saying he was going to move in with my father. My mom was crying. Everything was a disaster. I couldn't take it, so I ran upstairs to my room.

My dad moved out the Friday after he found a house to live in. I was so insecure about whether or not my parents would get back together. I would ask questions like, "Daddy, do you miss Mommy?"

He would always answer, "No, I don't."

Then I would ask questions like, "Daddy, do you have another girlfriend?"

And he would answer, "That's not something that is going to happen for a while."

After my dad moved out, my brother's anger got out of control. I even started to feel unsafe around him. He ended up moving in with my dad, thinking it would be better over there. But after a while, he saw that it was just the same.

I thought my dad moving out would make it so all the arguing would stop between my mom and him, but it didn't. Every time my dad would drop me off after coming home from his house, he and Mom would get into it with each other.

About six months after he moved out, I was surprised to find out that my dad had a girlfriend. She had a three-year-old that sometimes I just couldn't stand.

Then about eight months after my parents split up, Mom started seeing a guy she had been friends with her whole life. He had three boys. One of them was a year older than me, and another one was a year younger than me. I liked that I had someone to play with again. But after a while, they were always at our house, and I ended up not having any time to just spend alone with my mom anymore.

It seemed that nobody understood how I felt. I thought about running away and hoped that it would cure all of my sadness, but in my heart I knew that running away from my troubles wouldn't help anything.

I wanted to take my anger and sadness out on my dad, so I did some strange things to get back at him. For instance, I was offered the opportunity to go with friends on a trip to New York City, and another time they wanted to take me up to the mountains to learn how to ski. I turned them all down because somehow I thought that if I suffered, my dad would suffer, too, and I wanted my dad to realize he had ruined my life. The only thing that came of my behavior was that I didn't end up having any fun—and my dad never even noticed.

It's been two years since my dad moved out, and I have finally decided that I shouldn't sob and cry my whole life over something that I can't change. I only have one life, and if I spend it crying and sobbing, I can never get back the chance to just enjoy being a kid.

And since my parents split up, I have come to understand that no matter how much my parents fight—and who they choose to be with—it doesn't affect how much both of them still love me.

Karissa Porter, 12

Letting Go

You don't need strength to let go of something.
What you really need is understanding.

Guy Finley

On my seventh birthday, I received one of my favorite gifts ever—a pet guinea pig. His fur was soft as silk. He was white and light brown, with a jet-black head and beautiful black eyes. But it was because of the little black dots on his bottom that I named him Freckles. I loved him very much right from the start.

When I first got him, he was active and healthy. But as time passed, Freckles became less active and slept more. The only things this guinea pig really did a lot of were eat, sleep, and sit on his food bowl. But whenever anyone stepped into the room, Freckles would squeak and climb on the silver bars of his cage, which was sitting in the corner of the sunroom by the window.

On Freckles' third Christmas Eve, I went to cover

his cage with a blanket so that he wouldn't get too cold during the night. That's when I noticed how gooey his eyes were. I knew how dangerous it was for a guinea pig to get a cold, and I could tell that that was exactly what Freckles had. I picked him up and brought him to my mom. I told her that Freckles could die if we didn't do something. She said that he'd probably make it through this cold.

On Christmas day, I checked on Freckles to make sure he was still alive. He was, but he was barely holding on. Mom helped me put him into a box and wrap him up with towels to keep him warm. We saw to it that he was comfortable and had food with him, just in case he got hungry. As we opened presents, he sat by the vent, where heat was pouring out, and he started to get a little better. This lifted my spirits— until Mom looked at Freckles' cage, which I hadn't changed in a week. There were hardly any droppings, which meant that he hadn't been eating. Plus, his water bottle was still full. I started to cry. I knew that Freckles wasn't going to live through another Christmas.

That night, I brought Freckles into Mom's room where she and my aunt were playing a game. I took a handheld game and began playing it. Our games were interrupted by the sound of Freckles having trouble breathing. I wrapped him up tighter and whispered to him, "I love you very much, Freckles." Somehow he started to breathe more easily and even tried getting out of the box. I picked him up and stroked his beautiful, soft, furry back. Then Mom told me to put him back, so I did.

About five minutes later, Mom went to do a load of laundry. Freckles' breathing got faster and louder, and then it stopped. I quit playing solitaire and looked at him. His eyes were open, but the life had left his body. I felt a knot in my throat, and my eyes filled up with tears. I whispered, "He's . . . dead. . . ." My aunt looked at him and said, "I think you're right. The old guinea pig's time has finally come."

When Mom came back, she reminded me how miserable he had been and asked me if I really wanted him to live like that. I cried all night and most of the next morning. And when we buried him, I cried a little more.

It took a while to get used to the changes in the house after Freckles was gone. It was weird to be in the sunroom and not hear his playful squeaks or watch him play in his cage. I still have wonderful memories of Freckles, and I'll always remember him.

But the thing I'll remember most is that the hardest part of love is letting go.

Becca Sherman, 10

Granny's Hands

If we have the opportunity to be generous
with our hearts, ourselves, we have no idea
of the depth and breadth of love's reach.

Margaret Cho

My grandma was a generous person—not just to
my family and me, but to all kinds of people, even
people she didn't know. She did nice things without
ever expecting or wanting anything back. Over many
years, a lot of help passed through her hands and on
to others.

My grandma was especially good at baking. She
made the very best chocolate-chip cookies, which
were my favorite. But everyone in the family always
looked forward to her special pound cake when we
would get together.

One of the best things about my grandma was that
you could stop by and see her anytime, and she

would always welcome you. It didn't matter what she was doing; she would make time to visit with you.

When my friends would come to church with me, she would tell them to call her "Grandma," even though they were from totally different families. Then she'd give them a big, sloppy kiss on the cheek.

Everyone in our family always depended on Grandma to give us the news about the latest birth or who got married. Now she's not here to tell us what's going on, or to bake those favorite things she was so good at making, because my grandma passed away last summer.

She got cancer, and the doctors said they would be surprised if she lived another year. She didn't. She died about a month later. At least everyone got to see her one last time before she went to heaven.

During her funeral, my cousin started to read a poem, but he couldn't finish because it was too hard on him. About two weeks later, I found the poem. It described our grandma exactly.

Granny's Hands

Granny's hands used to touch me with such tenderness and care.
Granny's hands would scold me and sit me down in a chair.
Granny's hands would applaud me when I did something good.
Granny's hands would hold me every chance they could.
Granny's hands would aid me whenever I fell down.

Granny's hands, yes I miss them, they were the best hands around.

Granny's hands would spank me and say, "Now, baby, you act right."

Granny's hands would stroke me and tuck me in at night.

Granny's hands would pray for me, they would pray for all of us.

Granny's hands would rise in the air as in God she put her trust.

Granny's hands were special; they were the very best.

Granny's hands got tired, and now they are at rest.

Felicia Moore

I thought a lot about the last line of that poem. It taught me that it can be hard to lose people you love, but it can sometimes be for the better, too. When Grandma got sick, I felt so bad for her. I knew she couldn't do the things she loved anymore, and she was in pain. At least I know that she doesn't hurt anymore. I also realized that I never thought about how things would change once Grandma was gone. Losing someone you love can definitely help you appreciate the people who are special to you while you still have them in your life.

Victoria Williams, 12

HEATHCLIFF By George Gately

"Nobody pets him like Gran'ma."

It Isn't How It Used to Be

When I was born, she bathed my skin.

When I was one, she tucked me in.

When I was two, she blew the double candles on my cake out. Whew!

When I was three, she let me gallop on the "horse" that was her knee.

When I was so grown up at four, she coaxed me through the preschool door.

When I was five, she helped me keep our sickly, runty pup alive.

When I was six, I longed for storms and rainy weather, so we could snuggle up and read our books together.

Then seven. I can still recall the leaf prints that we made that fall. They're right up on my bedroom wall.

When I was eight, she started acting somewhat strange.

And last year was the time I noticed bigger things began to change.

And now I'm ten, and Grandma can't remember who
    I am . . . again.
I remind her, and she says, "I see," but I know when
    she looks at me, it isn't how it used to be.
I help her comb her snowy hair and go for walks
    whenever the air is still and warm, and read to her
    when there's a storm.
I coax her up the back hall stairs and say some silent
    prayers, and feel SO angry!
Uh-oh, here comes a tear, and Gran says, "What's the
    matter, dear?"
I bury my head in her shoulder and worry how it all
    will be when she and I are even older.
But anyway, I'm glad I came and that her hugs still
    feel the same.

Virginia L. Kroll

Two Good Teachers

On Monday, I smiled as Adam walked into my classroom carrying a big bag of guinea pig pellets.

"Squeaker is in his cage by the bookshelves," I said. "Mrs. Stewart tells me that you take care of him."

Adam looked away.

"She mentioned that you were going to build a maze for him. Do you still want to do that?" I continued. "You can if you like."

Adam hadn't made any effort lately to build the maze he had designed for Squeaker knowing that Mrs. Stewart wouldn't be there to see it.

When Adam arrived at the cage, I overheard him whisper to Squeaker, "I bet you wish Mrs. Stewart hadn't left," as he stroked the guinea pig's fur.

The next morning I instructed the class to spread out and make a circle so we could play Spelling Sparkle. Children spelled the week's assigned words one letter at a time, going around in a circle.

"I don't want to," Adam said to Kyle as he put away

his backpack. When it was his turn to spell, he messed up on purpose just so he could sit out.

Later that day, I walked over to Adam's table and said, "Mrs. Stewart told me that you like to build things."

"I used to," said Adam.

"My husband likes to work with wood. Could you use some wood scraps to make that maze?" I asked.

"I don't want to take care of Squeaker, and I don't want to go to school here anymore!" he fumed. I patted Adam's shoulder, but he pulled away.

During recess, I tossed a ball to Rachel.

"What a wonderful day to play catch! Who else wants in?" I asked.

"Not in a million years," I heard Adam mumble. "I promised Kyle I'd play basketball," Adam said. But I suspected he hadn't really promised anything.

After recess, I asked the students if anyone would like to e-mail Mrs. Stewart. "Just type in your message, and at the end of the day, we'll send them." Everyone thought this was a great idea. "Not me," said Adam.

That's when I knew that Adam was really hurting. I was sure he had a lot of questions for Mrs. Stewart, such as, "Why did you have to go back to college?" But it seemed he was too sad and maybe even a little mad at her for leaving.

The next morning when Adam walked into class, I held up a big green envelope. "We've got mail from Mrs. Stewart," I announced.

I let Carly open the envelope. There were photos of Mr. and Mrs. Stewart, their dog Petey, and their new home. Inside was a note that read:

> *Dear Children,*
>
> *I miss you! I know Mrs. Ingalls is very lucky to have such a good class. I like my college studies very much. I think of you often and say a prayer for you every day. Adam, please give Squeaker a carrot (but not celery) for me.*
>
> *Love,*
> *Mrs. Stewart*

That afternoon during recess, it seemed to me that Adam wanted to be alone. He walked to the swings and sat down. Slowly, I wandered over and sat in the swing next to his. For a long time, both of us were quiet.

"I thought Mrs. Stewart would be my teacher all year," Adam finally said as he dragged his feet in the sand, kicking up dust.

After awhile, I looked over at Adam and said, "People come in and out of our lives. And when that happens, new beginnings can be very hard. But Mrs. Stewart will never forget you, and I know you won't forget her either."

He blinked away a tear.

When the kids lined up after recess, I took Adam's hand and led him into the classroom. I pointed to a pile of wood scraps and a large piece of heavy cardboard placed on a table at the back of the classroom. A big bottle of wood glue sat straight and tall.

Adam looked surprised. He took a deep breath,

walked to his table, pulled the drawing he had made of the maze out of his red folder, and handed it to me.

Together, with the other children, we began building the maze Adam had planned.

While we worked, Adam suddenly looked up at me and said, "I'm lucky. I've had two nice teachers this year: Mrs. Stewart and you, Mrs. Ingalls."

Ann Ingalls

NO RODEO®

Pink Jelly Glasses

In this world of change, nothing which comes stays, and nothing which goes is lost.

Anne Sophie Swetchine

Little green apples blushed with pink hung from the leafy branches and waved in the breeze of a branch that spread over the front walkway of my grandpa's house. Scattered along the ground, decaying apples covered the walkway in a slimy mush. I had to clean the path to the house every day so that no one would slip and fall down. My dad would have done it, but he was so busy taking care of things now that Grandpa was gone that he said he didn't even have time to cry.

People came by the house in a steady stream, bringing coffeecake and hot casseroles. Cards came with the flowers, and kind words spilled from every direction. Everyone commented about the mess and suggested that the branch be trimmed, too.

The undertaker reported that an apple hit him on the head on his way down the path. Grandpa would have thought that was funny. He would have stroked my hair and called me his *bikku piika,* his little helper girl. I loved when Grandpa spoke in the old language to me. I wondered who would speak those special words to me now that Grandpa was gone.

One afternoon, while the adults were making plans for Grandpa's funeral, the neighbors came to visit and brought their granddaughter, Anna. She sat at the kitchen table, wriggling her fingers together while looking clearly bored. Finally, in a hushed voice, she asked if she could go outside with me to pick some apples. The thought of fresh air seemed tempting, so I agreed. We set out with two large sacks for collecting apples.

After a few minutes of picking, I realized that most of the apples were out of our reach. Then I spied the rake propped up next to the house, probably just where Grandpa had left it. He would have raked the yard after he mowed it with the old push mower. He never got to finish.

Oh, Grandpa, I miss you so much. I miss crawling up in your lap and hearing your funny stories. I miss your apple jelly. I miss hearing you laugh, I told him in my thoughts.

I picked up the rake, put it up into the tree, shook hard, and pulled at the branches. I wanted to scream out, "It isn't fair, and I want my grandpa-pa back!" I held back the tears and my words as I watched the ripe fruit fall.

I glanced around to see little Anna dodging falling apples. A few times, she got beaned in the head with one. That made me laugh, and it felt good after so much sadness. *Was I supposed to laugh during a time like this?* I wasn't sure.

We collected all the fallen apples, and then it was time for Anna to leave. I traded addresses with her so we could write to each other and stay friends.

The next day, Auntie Aila came over to the house and showed me how to make apple jelly. While we were pouring the jelly into the crystal-patterned jars, the phone rang. It was my best friend, Lisa. She wanted to see how I was holding up and to offer a best friend's advice on losing a grandpa. She said what I was feeling was normal, and that the tears would come. She also said that laughter was good. The best thing she said was that when her grandpa died, she took a pair of his glasses home with her. Then, whenever she missed him or was confused about something, she would put them on and try to see things through her grandpa's eyes.

After the funeral and the details were wrapped up, I realized that Grandpa was never coming back, and I finally cried. I looked over and noticed that Dad had begun to cry, too. I snuggled close in his arms as I told him what Lisa had said about it being okay to cry about losing Grandpa. I also told him about picking apples with my new friend, Anna. He said I was lucky to have two good friends—a new friend to help me laugh, and an old friend to remind me that it is okay to have all of these feelings.

Dad dried off both our tears with his sleeve and stroked his hand over my hair.

"Bikku piika," Dad said with a kind smile. "Thank you for reminding me that it's okay to cry."

When I packed my bags to return home, I added two jars of pink apple jelly to remind me of Grandpa. But next to the jelly jars was something that would last my lifetime and keep my grandpa in my heart forever—a pair of Grandpa's glasses.

Jacqueline J. Michels

Harry

*U*nderstanding is the first step to acceptance, and only with acceptance can there be
recovery.

J. K. Rowling

"Harry has to go," my mother said firmly. "That's all
there is to it."

I turned my back on her—slowly, deliberately—
and looked out to where our Doberman rushed
around the yard. He looked like a clown with the yellow collar the vet insisted he wear. I could imagine
how humiliating it must be and how it must itch. I'd
try to pull it off, too, if it were me.

I bit my lip as I thought of life without my best
friend. *How could Mom do this?* "You just don't care
about Harry anymore," I muttered. "You think he's
too big and too much trouble."

"That's not true, young lady," she said sharply.

"Maybe I shouldn't have gotten Harry in the first place. But I did, and now he's hurting himself almost every week trying to jump the fence. This yard is just too small."

I didn't think the yard was too small. It had always seemed an endless space with its fruit trees, the prickly forest of raspberry bushes, the large shed, and the huge walnut tree that towered over everything. Every corner of the yard reminded me of an adventure—and beside me, in every adventure, had been Harry.

Sometime later in the week, my mother announced she had found Harry a good home: a farm with acres for him to run in and where he had work to do. *Work? Why would Harry want to work when he could have fun with me?*

It wasn't long until I was out in the yard with Harry for the final time. The pain in my chest was so bad; I thought it would never go away. Harry, too, seemed to know it was our last day together. He walked slowly with his head down and his feet dragging through the grass. I was blinking to keep back the tears, angry at Mom and angry at Harry. "It's your fault," I told him. "If you hadn't kept jumping the fence, you wouldn't have to go."

At my harsh words, Harry looked up at me. His eyes were like little black pools, sad and helpless. I couldn't stand looking at him anymore, so I went back into the house.

Later, my older brother, Paul, came looking for me. "Aren't you coming? Don't you want to see Harry's new home?"

"You go. You think it's just great that Harry's leaving us," I said, my eyes never leaving the drawing I was coloring.

"Don't be so selfish," Paul said in that superior voice of his, like he was a hundred years older than me, not just two. "Harry will be much happier on a farm."

I didn't say anything, hoping he'd eventually give up and go away, which he did. I covered my ears when I heard the car start and pull away. I could block out any noise in the world, but I couldn't stop thinking of my last hurtful words to Harry. They followed me for days after.

"What's wrong with you?" Paul asked me one morning.

"Nothin'," I said sullenly.

"It's probably something stupid," Paul sniggered. "Did you lose one of your dolls again?"

I glared at him. "It's none of your business."

"It's none of your business . . . it's none of your business. . . ." Paul sang, mimicking my voice and dancing around my room.

"Oh, just be quiet!" I snapped at him. "I didn't lose a doll. . . . I lost Harry . . . and when he went, I told him it was all his fault. . . ." I could feel my eyes brimming over with tears, but this time I didn't try to stop them.

"Don't be such a baby," Paul said. "Harry's a dog— he wouldn't have understood what you said."

But I knew that wasn't true.

I woke up on Saturday to a funny feeling in the air. It seemed to crackle all around me like it did when there was going to be a storm, but the sun was out. I heard whispering as I walked down the hallway, but it stopped abruptly when I reached the dining room. My whole family was eating breakfast around the table, and they were all smiling at me. I could see Paul's feet dancing under the table as he struggled to keep still. His eyes gleamed at me with excitement. "We've got a surpri—"

"Shh!" Mom slapped his hand lightly.

I didn't ask what was going on. I didn't care about anything, unless it was Harry coming home. And so I didn't say anything when Mom ordered us into the car or when Dad drove us across the bridge and out into the country. We went past rolling hills topped with trees, miles of fields dotted with cattle and sheep, and winding creeks. Finally, we stopped.

"Come on!" Paul gave me a push as he jumped out of the car. I opened my door slowly and stood on the rough path. I stretched and breathed in deeply. The air was fresh and cool, and it seemed as though there was never-ending space, miles and miles of it.

My mother marched up to the gate that surrounded the house, and we all followed. A man near the house put down his bucket and walked slowly toward us. He gave a long, low whistle, and two dogs came running down from one of the far sheds. One of the dogs was a shaggy sheepdog, and the other was a Doberman who looked strangely familiar.

"Harry?" I called. I started running toward him, but then stopped as I watched how his long legs seemed to fly across the endless space between us. He could never have run like this in our backyard.

Harry danced around me and barked.

"He wants to show you around," the man said with a grin. "Why don't you go with him?"

So I did. I let Harry show me the sheds where the pigs burrowed in straw and the chickens laid their eggs, the paddocks where he rounded up sheep, and the veggie garden he helped to protect from wild animals.

I was still smiling when we all got back into the car. There was no need to feel upset and sad about Harry anymore. I realized that sometimes changes can be hard, but still be for the best. It helped when I finally saw that Harry was where he belonged.

Kristie Jones

6

LEARNING
TO FORGIVE

Forgiveness does not change the past, but it does enlarge the future.

Paul Boese

The Treasure

Forgiveness is a funny thing. It warms the heart and cools the sting.

William Arthur Ward

At six years old, I dreamed of becoming an artist. My mom knew this, and so she gave the perfect gift to a first-grade artist like me. My friends and I called them "Stampy Markers." They quickly became my treasure.

Unfortunately, my little sister thought they were amazing, too. For three days in a row, she would ask to play with my markers. Finally, she stopped asking, and I was able to leave them out in my room when I went to school, certain that she understood they were off-limits to her.

The first day that I didn't hide them, I got home from school and went upstairs to my room. Right away, I saw that my markers weren't where I had left them. My rainbow-colored treasures were gone!

Suspecting that my sister might have something to do with their disappearance, I searched the house for her. I found her in the basement and, sure enough, she was working on some rainbow drawing with my markers surrounding her.

I started yelling at her and grabbed the markers—at least the ones I could reach—and ran back up to my room, slamming the door behind me. I sat there for at least half an hour, but it seemed like much longer. Finally, I heard my sister's footsteps coming up the stairs.

I opened my mouth, about to demand that she give the rest of my markers back, when I noticed a folded piece of paper being pushed underneath the door.

Once it reached my side of the door, I picked it up. As I read the words written on the cover, my anger quickly fell away, and tears began to well up in my eyes. Then they began running down my cheeks. On the front of the paper in rainbow colors were the words "Best Sister." Inside was a picture she had drawn of herself offering me a late birthday gift.

How could I continue to be selfish and angry at her? How could I blame her for wanting to play with my markers? They were practically irresistible. And the fact that she used them to make something special for me made me realize that the greatest gift and treasure of all is the love you have for your family— and the love they have for you.

I opened the door, reached out to her, gave her a hug, and told her I forgave her.

As for the markers, they ended up running out of color or got lost; I'm not sure which. After all that happened, it didn't really matter. What matters is that I still have the best sister and the greatest treasure. After all, only love lasts forever, and that's the only treasure that everyone can share.

Charlotte Uteg

Keep Out

The summer I turned ten was one I'll never forget. It was the summer I crashed my bicycle and got a scar from my knee almost down to my ankle. It was the summer my best friend, Tasha, moved away, and we got our big, slobbery Saint Bernard. It was also the summer I discovered my brother's diary wedged between the wall and the turtle's tank.

If my brother had been anywhere in the house—or even in the yard—on the day I discovered it, I would have left it where it was. That day, however, my brother was at his friend's house, probably swimming in their pool, and I hadn't been able to find anyone to play with. It seemed so unfair, and I felt my brother was to blame. After all, he could have stayed home and played with me. Looking back, I can see that wasn't the greatest excuse.

I sat down on my brother's bed, on top of his *Star Wars* quilt, and pushed aside his stinky socks. I just held the black book with KEEP OUT scratched into the cover in my hands for a few minutes, watching our turtle, Emma, bask under the red heating lamp.

As Emma slipped off her rock into the murky water, I could no longer help myself, and I quickly flipped open the pages. For the most part, it was pretty disappointing: science homework due, a bad dream about living in a mushroom, the awful sweater he got from my grandma, and stuff like that. My brother didn't write much and had no real secrets—until I got to June 17.

The words on the page said, "I love Melissa."

The moment I read that, I knew I shouldn't have. I quickly shoved the diary back into place, went to my own room, and started reading. I didn't confront my brother; I just tried to forget all about it.

And I did forget all about the diary—for three weeks and five days. That day was the kind of summer day when you start to wish school was back on again because you have nothing to do.

My brother and I started nagging each other. Who knows what started it, but it got worse and worse until I was in tears. I was the one who *always* ended up in tears.

After my tears had dried, I knew what I was going to do. I was tired of being the one who lost every fight. I snuck my brother's diary out of his room and told my mom I was going for a bike ride.

I did go biking—straight over to Melissa's house. I showed her the diary and even went as far as saying that he wrote her name on everything and had carved a big heart with their initials in our tree house. Then I rushed back home to tell my brother what I had done.

As the color drained from my brother's face, I added that Melissa had said that my brother was "grody to the max," which was the worst thing I could think of. I didn't understand what that meant, but I had heard the big kids say it, and I was out to be the winner this time. I wanted my brother to end up in tears, the way I always did.

I can't even remember what my brother did to upset me that day, but I do remember the awful feeling I had from betraying a person that—although we fought—I loved. Even though my brother did end up in tears—tears of humiliation and anger—it didn't feel like I had won. In fact, it felt worse than, say, the embarrassment of having the most private secrets in your diary shared with everyone in the neighborhood.

Esme Sky Mills

The Tiny Bear

Have the courage to face the truth. Do the right thing because it is right. These are the magic keys to living your life with integrity.

W. Clement Stone

Aunt Evie had a miniature dollhouse. It was the most beautiful thing I had ever seen. Everything about it looked so real, as if tiny people had handcrafted each little doorknob and every piece of furniture.

Every Friday I went to Aunt Evie's because Friday was card night for my grandparents and their brothers and sisters. They would gather around in the dining room, eating pie and laughing, while I looked at the dollhouse for hours.

Sometimes I would pick up the delicate furnishings and place them in different positions. It was fun to decorate with the little items. Once, I asked Aunt Evie where she got the little miniatures so that I could buy some, too, one day. But Aunt Evie said that most of the miniatures were handcrafted and couldn't be replaced.

One such item was a small teddy bear an inch high. I was amazed by how beautifully it was sewn together. It was so tiny and had two little beads for eyes. I wanted the bear badly. *If I take it, Aunt Evie wouldn't even notice it's missing. But I could hold it in my hand and admire it all day long,* I thought to myself.

That Friday night, it took me a couple of hours to get the courage to take the bear and put it in my pocket. I had to wait until nobody was watching me. Once the bear was in my pocket, I couldn't wait to get home and look at it. I would have to hide it somewhere at home, so that no one would know I had it.

That night, I couldn't sleep. I tossed and turned and couldn't get comfortable. *What an awful person I am,* I thought. *I'm a thief, and I stole from my family.* When I woke up the next morning, I had a fever, but didn't seem to have a cold. I stayed in bed to punish myself for what I did. I couldn't tell my grandmother or Aunt Evie. I was too embarrassed about what I did. *There's no turning back,* I thought.

I felt worse and worse. My stomach started aching badly. I started hating the bear. I hated myself, too, and knew that if I didn't do something quickly, I wouldn't be released from the bad feelings I was having.

I decided to tell my grandmother. My hands were shaking, and I couldn't hold back the tears.

"I thought you knew better than to do something

like that." My grandmother shook her head in disappointment.

"I feel awful, Granny. I can't live with myself and what I've done," I said.

"There's only one way to make this right. You have to take the bear back and tell Aunt Evie what you did," she said.

I started to panic. Facing Aunt Evie and telling her that her niece was a thief was too much to ask. *Aunt Evie will never forgive me, and for the rest of her life, I will be embarrassed to look her in the face,* I thought.

"You're going to stand up and take the consequences for what you did, whether you like it or not," my grandmother said.

My finger was trembling when I rang Aunt Evie's doorbell. She opened the door as if she already knew what I was going to say. I showed her the little bear and told her I was sorry. Quietly, Aunt Evie picked up a box by the door and handed it to me. Inside was a miniature tea set.

"I admire your courage for coming here and returning the bear. You are my favorite niece even more now," Aunt Evie said.

During the ride home, I looked at the present on my lap. My stomach felt a lot better.

Lara Anderson

Mike's Trucks

The more you are willing to accept responsibility for your actions, the more credibility you will have.

Brian Koslow

"Hey, Sammy, see if you can come over to my house and play sometime," urged Mike.

"Okay, maybe I can come over Sunday," suggested Sammy.

"That would be great." Mike smiled. "I hope to see you then."

When he arrived home from school, Sammy asked his mother, "Mom, can I go over to my new friend Mike's house this Sunday?"

"Well, Sammy, I seem to remember that you promised Steve you would play with him on Sunday," Sammy's mother reminded him.

"Oops, I sort of forgot," Sammy thought out loud.

"Maybe Steve would want to come along, too."

In spite of Sammy's forgetfulness, it all worked out. Steve and Sammy both went to play with Mike on Sunday morning. It was Steve's idea that they play trucks. He had a toy dump truck for hauling dirt, and Sammy had a toy cement mixer.

When they arrived at Mike's house, Mike took both the boys out to his backyard and showed them his construction pit and all of his trucks. Mike's father had dug a small hole in the ground in their backyard and filled it with sand for Mike's work zone. In this huge sandbox, Mike not only had a cement mixer and a dump truck, but he also had a front-end loader, a crane, a bulldozer, a ditch digger, a road grader, and several other cool toys.

"Wow!" said Steve, his eyes opened wide. "Look at all *that!*"

Soon, the three boys were having fun building roads and digging holes with Mike's equipment. They used water from the garden hose and made a small lake in the bottom of the sand pit. But all too soon, it was time for dinner, and Sammy and Steve had to go home.

"Boy, those are really cool toys! I wish they were mine," Steve told Sammy as they left Mike's house.

Sammy didn't think much about what Steve said until a couple days later at school.

"You'll never guess what happened at my house," Mike said.

"What?" asked Sammy.

"Thieves broke into our backyard and stole my bulldozer and my ditch digger."

On his way home from school, Sammy got to thinking about what Steve had said: "Boy, those are really cool toys! I wish they were mine."

Surely Steve wouldn't have taken them, thought Sammy. But, just in case, he thought he should have a look for himself.

"Mom, can I go up to Steve's house to play?" asked Sammy.

"Sure, but don't be gone too long," said his mother. "You still have to do your homework."

"Okay, Mom, I'll be back in time," he assured her.

Sammy walked up to Steve's house. As he was about to knock on the door, he thought he heard Steve playing out in his sandbox. Sammy went around to the side of the house and peeked around the corner. Sure enough, there was Steve. And there was Mike's bulldozer and his ditch digger, too!

"Hi, Steve. I thought I'd come over and play trucks with you," Sammy announced.

"Oh!" Steve seemed startled. "I didn't hear you coming."

Steve could tell by the look on Sammy's face that he knew.

"Why did you take Mike's toys?" Sammy asked.

Steve just hung his head.

"Steve, it's wrong to steal," he said. "Mike will share his toys with us any time we go to his house."

"But what can I do now? I can't just take them back," said Steve.

"Well, that's what you need to do," Sammy assured him. "Come on, I'll go with you."

After asking both their moms' permission, the two made their way to Mike's house with the trucks.

"You found my trucks! Where were they?" shouted Mike when he opened the front door.

"I took them," Steve confessed.

"You mean *you* were the burglar?" Mike asked. He seemed really shocked.

"Yeah, it was me," admitted Steve.

"Why?" asked Mike.

"I don't know. All I know is that I'm sorry," Steve said.

After a few seconds, Mike said, "It's okay, Steve. I forgive you."

Steve reached out to Mike, and the two shook hands. With a smile breaking on their faces, the three of them ran back to Mike's backyard and played until it was time to go home.

Ronnie Reese

Trouble in Neverland

The clock struck twelve, and my third-grade class-mates and I ran from our desks and out the door. It was time for recess, the only part of the day anyone really cared about. Jamie, my best friend, was also in my class, and as soon as we hit the playground, we ran to the farthest basketball court. No one played there. If they wanted to play basketball, they would usually play on the court closest to the water foun-tain. Kickball was also a popular sport, and if you weren't playing kickball, you were probably on the swings and slides. Since no one played at the farthest basketball court, Jamie and I could play whatever we wanted and not have to worry about anyone com-plaining or interrupting our game.

We liked to pretend we were in different places, like the jungle, the desert, or off in some fairytale world. One day, we decided to play Peter Pan.

"All right, here is where Wendy lives," I said, point-ing to a four-square section of the court. "And Peter

Pan will live near that basketball hoop." Jamie liked my idea and started to make up our situation.

"Peter will be in trouble, so Wendy has to come in the middle of the night and save him," Jamie told me.

"That sounds good. . . . I think I'm going to be Tinker Bell," I said. Suddenly Jamie looked at me.

"But I want to be Tinker Bell. . . ." she complained.

I told her that I'd thought of the idea first, but she still whined.

"Come on, Jamie . . . you can be Tinker Bell tomorrow," I said, hoping she would drop it.

"No! I'm going to be Tinker Bell today. It's only fair," she yelled.

"How is it fair?" I asked.

"It just is!"

I sighed. This fight was going nowhere. "Okay," I said, "either I get to be Tinker Bell, or we won't play this game at all."

"Wow!" Jamie yelled. "Not only is that a stupid idea, but its mean, too! I guess that's how Jewish people are." She walked away.

I stared at her back and watched her walk toward the swings. *What happened? What does me being Jewish have to do with the both of us wanting to be Tinker Bell?* I knew that it really didn't mean anything, but it still wasn't a right or nice thing to say. Just then, the teachers blew their whistles, and recess was over.

I told my teacher that Jamie and I had gotten into a fight, and she let us talk outside the classroom. The talk was useless. Jamie didn't seem to care that she had hurt my feelings. I didn't know how much it had hurt until I realized I was yelling at her. I stopped and told her I was sorry.

"It's okay. What I said was really rude. I shouldn't have said it. I guess I'm the one that's sorry," she said.

"Thank you," I whispered.

"No problem. And I promise never to say anything mean about your religion again. Do you forgive me?" she asked.

"Of course, I forgive you!" I laughed, taking her hand and walking back into the classroom.

Jamie and I stayed best friends until middle school, when we went to different schools and eventually drifted apart. But I'll never forget her or the fact that she never did insult my religion again, just as she promised.

Carly Hurwitz

All Because of Kelly

True friendship is like sound health; the value of it is seldom known until it is lost.

Charles Caleb Colton

Liz and I have been best friends for as long as I can remember. We're neighbors, and we're in fourth grade, and we both have the same teacher. We have done everything together, from building sand castles at the beach, to having sleepovers and going on camp-outs. We have also shared all of our secrets with each other. But our friendship almost ended a few days ago.

It all started with the new girl. Her name is Kelly. She came to school a month ago, and she's already ruined my life.

Nobody is perfect, but Kelly *looks* perfect. She has blonde hair, bright blue eyes, and a perfect smile, too. She is also very smart.

One thing that really makes me mad is to see her whispering to Liz in the hallway at school. When I get close to them, Liz looks embarrassed, and Kelly laughs, like she's talking about me and maybe saying things that aren't true. Then they're really quiet and wait for me to leave.

Maybe Kelly just likes Liz, and she wants to take her away from me so they can be friends. I still don't understand why we can't all be friends. That's what I thought, anyway.

At first, it didn't seem that bad, but then, at lunch, Kelly started taking *my* seat next to Liz. So I took an empty chair and put it next to her. They pretended not to notice me. When I think about it, it seems like a long time ago, even though it happened just a couple of weeks ago. I guess it seems like forever because I miss Liz so much. About that same time, I let Kelly use my mechanical pencil. I don't know why, because she is always so mean to me, but I thought that if I was nice to her then, maybe she would be nice back. She gave the pencil back to me broken.

Since Kelly came to school, Liz has changed toward me. Last week at school, during free time, when I asked her if she wanted to play cards, all she said was, "No, I can't. Sorry. Kelly and I are going to play checkers." When I asked Liz if I could play, too, she said that it's only for two players, and they wanted to be alone.

When I heard that, I was so hurt that I couldn't stand it. I wasn't only mad that Liz was playing with Kelly every day and ignoring me. I was also mad because Kelly had totally changed Liz. Now, her personality was bratty and mean. She always used to share, but now she didn't.

This is the hardest part of the story to tell. Two days ago, Liz came up to me at school and said she needed to talk to me after lunch. At first, I thought it was probably a joke that she and Kelly were going to play on me. Then I thought that maybe she would say she was sorry and ask if I would be her friend again. All during lunchtime, I was excited, and I kept my hopes up.

After lunch, instead of Liz saying she was sorry and asking if I could ever forgive her, she said, "Listen, I know we've been friends for a long time, but now I think it's time to find some other friends, and I think it would be better if we weren't friends anymore."

As soon as I heard that, I started feeling tears in my eyes, but I didn't want to cry in front of her. When she left, I spent the whole afternoon trying not to cry. So that's how it happened. Liz and I haven't hung out with each other for a couple of days now.

Just now, as I finished writing this story in my bedroom, I heard a knock on the door. When I opened it, I was very surprised to see Liz. We stared at each other for almost a minute, and then she hugged me and said she was *so* sorry, and that she's never felt as terrible in her whole life as she has the last couple of days.

After she apologized, she said that she just wanted to be popular, and that Kelly said she could only be friends with her. I told her, "Liz, you don't have to be popular to be happy. You just have to do what you want and be with the friends you want. . . . You're my best friend, Liz, and I forgive you."

Then Liz said the best thing I've heard in three weeks: "You're my best friend, too." After Liz apologized and we were friends again, I went back to my room to finish this story about Liz and me, and I was glad it had a happy ending. When I think about it, if it weren't for Kelly, Liz and I would never know our true feelings of friendship. In a way, I really thank her. When I finished writing this story, I went back to put the title on it: *All Because of Kelly.*

Amy Cornell, 10

"Well, that was the last of the grudges
I've been holding."

Reprinted by permission of Jonny Hawkins. ©2006 Jonny Hawkins.

Forgiving My Dad

In this world it is not what we take up, but what we give up, that makes us rich.

Henry Ward Beecher

I was seven years old and my little brother was only four on the day my parents told us they were going to get a divorce. I couldn't believe it. I remember every detail of that day. They had taken us to a park by a little stream for a picnic. It was a nice, sunny day, and the spot was really beautiful. We were sitting under a big oak tree when they told us. My parents must have thought that if they took us somewhere nice, maybe the bad news wouldn't be so hard for us to accept. *Yeah, right.*

When they told us they wouldn't be living together anymore, I cried. So did my brother, but I don't think he really knew why. I remember thinking, *How could they do this to us? What is going to happen to us? Was it our fault? They said it wasn't our fault, and they both still loved us very much. If they did, why were they doing this?* Dad told us we would live with him. I found it very hard to understand.

We moved away from the town that we used to live in as a family—just me, my brother, and our dad. I know it was just as hard for our dad to accept as it was for us. Sometimes, I would walk into the bedroom of our small place and find Dad crying. I hated to see him like that. He tried to hide it from us as much as he could, but you could tell he'd been crying because his eyes were red. I pretended not to notice.

My brother missed Mom a lot, and he cried a lot, too. I did my best to be there for him, and I tried to help Dad by cooking things for dinner—simple things like beans on toast. I don't know if it helped much, but I didn't know what else I could do. I would also get my brother ready for school and clean up our bedroom in the morning, so Dad wouldn't have to.

After a few months, Dad told us we would have to go and live with our grandparents for a while. He said he had to go back to college to get his degree so he could get a better-paying job in order to take care of us. At the time, I was so upset and angry. *How could he leave us after we had already lost our mom? He had told us we would live with him!*

We had to take a plane to where our grandparents lived because it was so far away. Our grandparents were pleased to see us, as always, but this time they were especially welcoming. This was going to be our home for a while. It came time for Dad to leave, but I didn't want him to go. He told us he wouldn't be able to visit as often as he would like because he would be very busy at the university. As I watched him walk away, I couldn't believe he was leaving us. *It was bad enough that Mom was gone, but now Dad, too?*

He visited us every couple of months for a few days at a time. It was always hard when he had to leave because we weren't sure when we were going to see him again. Sometimes we would take a flight, just my brother and me, to spend a few days with him. The flight attendants were always really nice to us. But it seemed that by the time we got to Dad's, we had to turn around and go back to our grandparents' house. The visits were never long enough.

Finally, after three years of living with my grandparents, Dad came to visit for the last time. He had finished school, and found a good job and a nice place for us to live. I had missed him for so long that I cried when he told us we'd be living together again and that he was finally taking us home!

When we are kids, we don't really understand why our parents do some of the things they do. I didn't really understand why my dad had to leave us for so long or why we couldn't just stay with him. But he made the difficult choice of having his parents look after us so he could get a better education and find a better job. It was very hard for him, too, but he did the right thing.

Now I understand that what he did, he did for us.

Sarah McIver

7

SHARING
AND GIVING

My mom says it's good to share,
From crayons to my favorite chair.
I'm not too sure I think it's fun.
Still, I give to everyone.
I have one friend who I don't mind,
To give a lick on what I've dined.
Bandito's sweet and not a hog.
He's my best friend and my dog.
But, boy, did Mommy ever groan,
When I shared my ice-cream cone.
Bandito hardly made a drip,
And even ate the minty chip!

Sandra Green

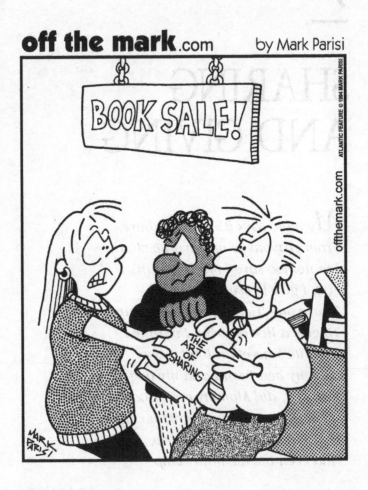

Making Friends with a Puppet

Life has taught me that respect, caring, and love must be shared, for it's only through sharing that friendships are born.

Donna Favors

The first thing I noticed was her hair. It was black and long and shiny, like my music teacher's piano. I thought she looked like a princess from a faraway country. She stood all alone at the edge of the school playground.

"Who is she?" I asked my teacher. I aimed a nod at the girl.

"She's the new girl in Mrs. McNair's class," my teacher said. "She's from a migrant worker family. They don't speak English—only Spanish."

I didn't know anything about migrant workers, but I did know a few Spanish words. I knew that *uno, dos, tres,* meant one, two, three. I knew *adios* meant good-bye. *If I could get those words right,* I thought, *I could talk to that girl.*

I walked toward her, my mouth as dry as the playground's sandbox. I stopped a few steps away from her. She looked up at me. I opened my mouth, but the words were all wrong. *What kind of conversation is "one, two, three, good-bye"?* I turned and ran. For the rest of recess, I watched her from the safety of the tetherball line.

Every day, she stood in the same spot on the edge of the playground, and every day, I tried to think of something to say or do. The easiest thing to do was to pretend I didn't see her, just like all the other kids did. But doing this bothered me.

A couple weeks later, I moped into Mom's bedroom one afternoon. She was making felt puppets for the church bazaar. I picked up the black yarn Mom was using for the puppets' hair. It reminded me of the new girl's shiny hair.

"Mom, can I make a puppet?" I said.

"Sure," Mom said.

I used tan felt for the puppet's skin and long, shiny black yarn for its hair. Mom helped me find two brown buttons for the eyes. That night, I went to sleep with the puppet tucked under my pillow and a plan tucked in my head.

The next day, I could hardly wait until recess. Spelling seemed to take forever. When the bell finally rang, I ran outside with the puppet. I saw the girl standing in her usual spot. I pulled the puppet out of my pocket and slipped it over my hand. I hurried across the playground and sat next to the new girl.

"Hello," said the puppet (in my voice). "Want to play with me?"

I handed her the puppet and helped her slip it on her hand.

At first, the puppet moved without saying anything. Then, it spouted spicy words that danced into my ear. The words made no sense to me, but one word jumped out from the others. "Luisa," the puppet said. "Luisa." She handed the puppet back to me.

"Hello, Luisa. This is Erika," I said, making the puppet point to me. "She wants to be your friend."

We took turns with the puppet for the rest of recess. When I held the puppet, it spoke English, and when Luisa did, it spoke Spanish. The bell rang. Luisa tried to give me the puppet, but I pushed it toward her. "It's for you," I said.

Luisa's smile warmed me inside. It was the kind of smile I knew I'd never forget.

The next day, I ran outside at recess and looked for Luisa. She wasn't there. The next day was the same. She was gone. I found Mrs. McNair refereeing a four-square game.

"Where's Luisa?" I asked.

"Her family moved again," she said.

"But she just got here," I protested.

Mrs. McNair shrugged.

I turned and wandered toward the edge of the playground. I stood in the spot where Luisa used to stand. I was glad she had the puppet. And I was glad I had the memory of Luisa's smile.

Lana Krumwiede

The Joy of Giving

Neither fire nor wind, birth nor death can erase our good deeds.

Buddha

I was eleven when my grandparents and I fled our country, Hungary, with only the clothes on our backs. We ended up in a refugee camp, also called a displaced persons camp, where we joined throngs of other refugees who had arrived before us.

Our new home was made up of old army barracks that were lined up like soldiers as far as the eye could see. Although the camp was cramped, it was an improvement over the life we had known in our war-torn country for several years.

Soon after our arrival, we were taken to one of the barracks that would serve as our new home. They had small rooms with sleeping cots, a blanket covering the entrance, and not much more. But I was grateful for the "safe" roof over my head, and the warm soup they served us.

Soon, a girl with long, curly black hair came over and introduced herself.

"Hi, my name is Piri, and I sleep on the other side of the cardboard wall, so we're neighbors," she said, smiling at me. I liked her instantly.

"Nice to meet you," I said. "My name is Renie, and I'm eleven. How old are you?"

"I'm nine-and-a-half," Piri replied, "and I can show you around the camp. We've been here over a year now."

So Piri and I became friends, and although I soon made friends my own age, I let her hang around with us. It was nice to have someone look up to me and admire me just because I was older. And it was comforting to have her on the other side of the cardboard wall at night so I could tell my problems to her.

Because most of us in the camp had no money, we looked forward to the donated clothes they gave to us each spring and fall. And if the clothes came from America, we fingered them in awe, for that is where most of us hoped to go.

Of course, the clothes weren't new, but they were clean and good, and we were grateful to get them. This also meant that no one looked better than anyone else at camp.

One winter morning, we had lined up to receive our winter clothes when the man in charge made an announcement.

"This year, a rich lady in America donated this beautiful fur coat in a young girl's size." He held up the coat for everyone to see. *Oohs* and *aahs* rang out through the crowd.

"Since we only have one coat and many young girls, we have decided to have a drawing for it. Girls will come up and try it on, and if the coat fits, they will write their name on a piece of paper and drop it in this box. Then we will draw the name of the winner."

"That coat looks like it will fit you perfectly," my grandmother said. "Go try it on, and put your name in the box."

"It looks too big for me," Piri said. "But I will keep my fingers crossed that you win the coat. It would look beautiful on you."

So I went and felt the coat. It was soft, plush, and lovely to the touch, and I wanted it very badly. So did many of the other girls. And after what seemed like forever, a small girl was asked to reach into the box and draw a name.

"Renie Szilak," the man shouted, waving a piece of paper in the air. "Come on up here, young lady, and get your coat."

I stood there in a daze, not quite believing it was true until Piri nudged me on. I walked up, feeling the hundreds of eyes watching me. And when I walked back, wearing that beautiful coat, I heard a voice in the crowd call out, "You look just like a real princess in that coat!" It was the cutest boy in our school. I blushed, but I hoped I was walking the way a real princess would.

"I can't believe some girl in America gave up this coat," I told Piri as we walked back to our barrack.

"Maybe it no longer fit her," Piri said.

"But it is so beautiful. I won't give it up even after it no longer fits. It will be mine forever!" I vowed.

By this time, Piri had become the closest thing to a sister I would ever have. Since her father was sick and needed her mother at his side most of the time, she spent much of her time with my family and me. And since both of our families had applied for immigration to the United States, a lot of that time was taken up with dreaming about our future lives there.

"I hope we'll be neighbors in America and always be friends," Piri would often say.

"I hope so, too," I would add.

That winter, I felt like a refugee-camp princess. Everywhere I went in my new coat, admiring glances followed, and when I walked to school, boys who usually threw snowballs at the girls let me walk by untouched.

Then spring arrived, and I put the coat in a box and shoved it under my sleeping cot. But I knew it would be there for me next winter.

Not long after, we received the news we had been awaiting. Our papers had been approved, and in September we would board the ship taking us to our new country: the United States of America. I rushed out to find Piri and tell her the good news, thinking their papers had come through, too. I found her outside the barrack, her eyes red from crying.

"What's wrong?" I asked.

"We haven't been approved. They say my dad is sick. Only healthy people can go to America," she replied quietly, turning my world upside-down.

"Oh, I am sorry," I said, putting my arms around her, wishing I could do something more to help her. We spent the remaining few months practically glued to each other, but soon the day we had to part arrived.

Piri and I were about to say our last farewell before my family and I boarded the truck that would take us to the ship.

"Don't forget me. Write to me," Piri said, hugging me as tears rolled down her cheeks. Suddenly, it hit me hard that not only would we never see each other again, but Piri would not be going on to a new life in a new country. I had to somehow ease her sadness. I broke away from the crowd and ran after my grandfather, who was just boarding the truck with a large box in his hand. I yanked the box from him without an explanation and raced back to Piri's side.

"I want you to have the coat. I love you, little sister, and I'll write as soon as we have an address," I said tearfully, shoving the box into her hands.

"But . . . but you said you would never give up this coat," Piri stammered.

"I'm not giving it up. I'm passing it on to my little sister. Think of me whenever you wear it."

Then I raced to climb aboard the truck, which was about to depart without me. I will never forget the expression on Piri's face as she stood there clutching the box, teetering between sadness and gladness. That was the moment that I, a mostly selfish girl, discovered how much joy there is in giving.

It was mid-November by the time I could send my address to Piri. I received her happy reply just a few days before Christmas. There was a photo enclosed in the letter, too. It showed a girl with curly black hair and a beaming smile. She wore a beautiful fur coat, and she looked just like a real princess it.

And that made my heart happy.

Renie Burghardt

To Give Love

A kind and compassionate act is often its own reward.

William Bennett

When I was a child, our house was next door to the Schonfield Home. It was a place where people who got too old to take care of themselves lived. I was a regular visitor and volunteer there. I enjoyed spending time with the wonderful, caring staff and the residents who always seemed happy to see me.

One older lady named Mrs. Kurtz always seemed to be sad. I had never seen her smile or laugh like the other residents. No one ever came to visit her, or sent her cards or flowers. My parents explained to us that we must be extra nice to her since she had no family or friends. They felt that the reason she did not smile was because she was all alone in the world.

One day, I was visiting the home, and I saw Mrs.

Kurtz sitting alone, looking very upset. I asked one of the other residents, Mrs. Smith, why Mrs. Kurtz was more depressed than usual. Mrs. Smith explained to me that Mrs. Kurtz had turned eighty-nine, and she was upset to be celebrating another birthday all alone without anyone or even any cards or gifts. She truly believed there was no one in the world who loved her.

This moved me deeply, and I started to hatch a plan in my mind. I ran home and raced to my room. I poured out all the money in my bank that I had received on birthdays and other occasions. Until now, I had been saving money for a new bike. Although it wasn't enough for a bike, it was enough for what I wanted to do now.

I raced down the stairs and explained to my mother what I was about to do, and she smiled at me proudly. She planted a kiss on my cheek and said, "I must be the luckiest mother in the world to have such a caring daughter."

My mother stopped what she was doing, and we went to a gift shop where we picked out a lovely heart-shaped musical jewelry box. Our next stop was the card store where we bought a birthday card to go with the gift. Then we went to the florist and bought a beautiful bouquet of red roses.

Then I wrote the following in the card:

> To the best lady at Schonfield Home, happy birthday and all the best!
> From your neighbor who loves you very much, Mimi

With all our gifts, we headed for the home, and as expected, we found Mrs. Kurtz still sitting alone and looking very sad. But the minute we approached her and gave her our gifts, I saw her eyes widen in surprise. As she finished reading my message on the card, she looked up and flashed the first smile she had ever given to me.

When I said good-bye to her a while later, Mrs. Kurtz was still smiling, and at that moment, I noticed that my heart was smiling along with hers.

Mimi Frid

"My brother Louie finally learned to share.
He gave me his chicken pox."

Fifty-Six Grandparents

*You must give some time to your fellow men.
Even if it's a little thing, do something for
others—something for which you get no pay
but the privilege of doing it.*

Albert Schweitzer

There was my mother, standing in a fuzzy pink bunny
costume, holding a basket of eggs. *This can't be happening,*
I thought to myself. Being ten was hard enough.

I had begged to stay home that day, complaining
I'd caught some rare disease and needed to stay in
bed. My mother, who's a nurse, looked me over and
sent me to school anyway. It was the day our fourth-
grade class was taking a field trip to sing to the residents of a nearby convalescent home.

When we got there, I stood at the front door with
my entire fourth-grade class, secretly wishing for that
rare disease. I'd fall to the ground, be rushed away,

and spared the humiliation of anyone ever knowing that I spent every day after school there—me and my mother, the Easter Bunny.

"Hi, Shelly!" The residents waved and smiled as we entered.

"Do you know them?" Angela asked, disgusted.

"No!" I replied. "They're just old and confused. They probably think I'm someone else. Besides, my name's Machille, not Shelly," I reminded her sarcastically.

The men and women who lived in the convalescent home were lined up outside their rooms. Most of them sat in wheelchairs, some stood behind walkers, and some had been wheeled out in their beds.

My mother had explained to me many times that these were special people. Now that they were older and needed a nurse's care for different reasons, they lived here with each other. I thought of it more like a "grandparents' pound"—forgotten grandparents. I saw who had visitors and who didn't.

Our class started singing, and I studied my shoelaces. If I looked up, I might make eye contact with one of them. Everything was going well until Mrs. Deist, our teacher, handed me four tulips that we were supposed to give to the residents. I quickly went to the back of the line. My mother didn't say a word to me; she just went along her way—hopping.

Last year, she had made a red bunny costume for me and we hopped down the halls together, laughing and singing. It had been a lot of fun. *But I'm too old for that now*, I thought.

I shuffled behind my class and gave my tulips to other classmates. They didn't ask any questions, just took the flowers.

"What are you little brats doing here?" Hattie May barked out, snatching a tulip from Jacob's hand.

Hattie May had been here for years. She had a disease that made her forget things and sometimes made her grumpy. She always liked me, though. Sometimes she called me Susie, but I didn't mind. My mom told me her daughter's name is Susie. I've seen Susie before—she's my mom's age, but Hattie's disease doesn't understand time.

Jacob's face turned bright red. The class giggled and pointed. My teacher did her best to keep us moving, knowing that Hattie May didn't mean any harm. I heard someone whisper, "Crazy old lady." The sinking feeling in the pit of my stomach got worse. I smiled at Hattie May as we passed, and she smiled at me.

"Shelly, how about a game of Fish?" Lou grinned, grabbing my arm.

My class and teacher turned and stared. I pulled my arm away and whispered to Lou, "Later, okay?"

I didn't look up; I just waited for the feet in front of me to start moving again. But they didn't move. I studied the tile floor, thinking how cold the floor seemed with the bright lights reflecting off of it. Now I felt like I was officially the "freak show."

"Machille, do you know these people?" Mrs. Deist asked me.

"Um . . . I . . . kinda . . ." I mumbled.

"Well, then, you should lead the way," she smiled and handed me a bunch of tulips.

Could it get any worse? I thought. As I moved to the front of the line, I could hear the rest of the class muttering under their breath. I know they were all talking about me, probably saying things like, "Well, she doesn't have any other friends; why shouldn't she hang out with a bunch of old people?"

I pulled up my chin and looked straight ahead. In front of me were rows of familiar and loving faces. They all smiled big, warm, real smiles. I couldn't help but smile back. I stepped forward and handed a tulip to Rose, a white-haired woman standing behind her walker.

"How's the hip feel today, Rose?" I asked with a grin.

"Okay, Shelly. Thanks for asking," Rose answered and squeezed my hand.

I suddenly forgot that the class was watching me. I continued down the hall, waved to Frank, and gave Mr. Blusso a high-five. When I was out of tulips, I turned back to Mrs. Deist, who handed me five more. Other kids had stopped and were talking with the patients. I saw Angela laughing as Frank showed her a card trick. Jacob was covering Mr. Blusso's legs with a blanket. Mrs. Deist put her arm around me and pulled me close.

"My mother was in a convalescent home for five years before she passed away. I wish she'd had someone like you to look in on her when I couldn't be there. You're very special, Machille," Mrs. Deist winked.

My mother picked that moment to hop over and thank us all for coming by. I proudly took her by the hand and introduced her to my class.

"This is my mom, Geneva. She works here, and every day she takes care of all these special people." I stood tall and straight as I delivered the information. The whole class began to clap.

"Wow. My mom would never put on a bunny costume. Your mom is cool," Tom said, slapping me on the back.

"Hey, do you think I could come by sometime with you after school? I really like that guy Lou, and he promised to teach me how to play gin rummy," Jacob asked.

"Me, too, Machille?" Angela chimed in.

My mother spoke before I could and explained about a program where kids can volunteer after school and on the weekends. The patients cheered at the idea, and my class seemed very excited, too.

That day, I realized how happy it made me to make other people smile and feel good. I should never be ashamed of that. I also learned how lucky I am. I have fifty-six grandparents.

Machille Legoullon

Esperanza

The first time my fifth-grade class found out about Hope was the day I wore my new "Hope Bracelet." It was a beautiful, dainty bracelet made of shiny pink beads, and in small silver letters it spelled out the name HOPE. Hope was a first-grade girl from a neighboring town who, along with her mother, was suffering from cancer. I explained that the bracelets were being made and sold by a family friend in order to help Hope's family with the cost of their care.

I could always count on this fun-loving group of students to take part in our group discussions, but this time, something was different. The students were paying close attention and asked lots of questions about Hope and cancer in general.

During the discussion, one of the twenty students announced that she would like to order a Hope Bracelet. Then, another girl joined her, and then another. Hands were going up right and left when suddenly a boy said over the crowd, "I want one, too! I don't care if they're pink; I want to help Hope." Before long, we had an order for twenty Hope Bracelets.

The next day, the class was full of pride and bubbling over with excitement when a short math lesson revealed that together we had raised close to ninety dollars for Hope and her family. Then, just like the day before, the students started raising their hands again. This time they were asking: "Mrs. Abbott, could we have a car wash or a bake sale to raise more money for Hope?"

I knew that these types of projects weren't the kind of activities that we could do in the classroom, so I needed to come up with a plan.

With our principal's permission, the next day I announced that we were going to have a read-a-thon for Hope. The students would read all they could for the month of February. They would find family and friends who would sponsor them at a penny a page for what they read during the month. At the end of the month, the students would collect their money, and we would put it all together and present it to Hope. The enthusiasm spread fast as the students built up their lists of sponsors. A group of volunteers who were already helping our school with a special reading program signed up. To get more support, one family member took a sponsor sheet to a local hospital, where Hope's father worked.

The read-a-thon was moving in the right direction. Along with outside reading, if we read five pages out of the social studies book, seven pages out of the literature book, or two pages out of the grammar book, the students would record each of these pages on their individual reading log.

One of our favorite activities was reading from our class novel. I had received this book a year earlier, but until then hadn't gotten around to reading it to them. Each day, after lunch, I would say to the class, "Let's read for Hope now." Then, I would pick up *Esperanza Rising,* by Pam Muñoz Ryan, and begin reading. It was a fabulous novel that took us on a journey with a young girl, named Esperanza, who endured many challenges and obstacles only to come out stronger in the end.

We enjoyed the novel so much each day that we were sad to see it come to an end. To make it last a little longer, we read the "About the Author" page at the end of the book. You cannot imagine how shocked we were when we read the very last line: "It is no wonder that, in Spanish, *esperanza* means . . ."

Suddenly, the breath was sucked out of me, and I had to gulp like a swimmer coming up for a desperate breath of air. With tears filling my eyes, I collected myself and repeated, "It is no wonder that, in Spanish, *esperanza* means 'hope.'"

In April of that year, my forever-changed class surpassed their initial contribution of ninety dollars and proudly presented Hope and her dear family a check for $1,310.44.

Angela Abbott

A Healing Haircut

There are two primary choices in life: to accept conditions as they exist, or accept the responsibility for changing them.

Denis Waitley

It was about ten o'clock in the evening when I crept across the kitchen floor. My feet seemed to make a whole lot of noise. Luckily for me, Mom was on the phone, so she wouldn't immediately send me back to bed. I had an *American Girl* magazine clutched to my chest, my finger marking a certain page. I waited behind a wall until Mom was off the phone before walking into the room.

"Mom," I called softly as I walked in.

She looked at me, so I knew she was listening.

"Mom, you know how you want me to cut my hair? Well, now I want to do it, and I want to send my hair here...." I said, and I showed her the article I had read about Locks of Love.

Locks of Love is a company that takes donations of hair, makes the hair into wigs, and gives the wigs to kids who are suffering from a disease or accident that make them lose their own hair. Locks of Love provides the wigs at almost no cost.

Until I read the article, I had always insisted on keeping my hair long. Now I wanted to cut it short. Mom looked shocked.

"Are you sure you want to do this?" Mom asked.

"Yes, I am," I answered seriously.

"Why?" Mom asked.

"When I read that article," I began, "I thought of all those kids who need my hair more than I do. I knew I had to help them."

Mom gave me a hug and told me how proud she was that I was doing this.

The next day, Mom called the number in the article for more information.

"You need ten inches of hair or more," she informed me when she got off the phone. Mom measured my hair with a ruler. "You have twelve inches!" she told me.

Two weeks later, I went to get my hair cut. I told Jenny, the stylist, what I wanted to do.

First, she washed my hair, and then she cut it. She told one of the other stylists to put it into a bag. She gave it to me before we left.

When we got home, Mom told me to set my hair on the dining-room table to dry in the sunlight that came in from the window. It took about a week. When my hair was finally dry, Mom and I wrapped gold ribbons around it and sent it off to the address Locks of Love had given us. I had typed up a letter asking that my hair go to a burn victim. My mom had told me horror stories about when she worked in the burn unit, and I felt especially sorry for them.

I was very proud of what I did. I knew some child, probably a girl, was delighted, at least for the moment. She would be wearing a wig with curly brown hair.

A few months later, I got a thank-you card. I didn't need it. The good feeling I got doing it was thanks enough. I learned that acts of love aren't just hugs and kisses, but that thoughtful gestures to complete strangers are acts of love, too.

Angela Rooker

[EDITOR'S NOTE: *If you're interested in donating hair to Locks of Love, go to www.locksoflove.org for information on how to make your donation. Following are the charity's guidelines for donation hair:*

1. *Ten inches minimum hair length (tip to tip). They cannot accept wigs, falls, or synthetic hair.*
2. *Please bundle hair in a ponytail or braid.*
3. *Hair needs to be clean, dry, placed in a plastic bag, then in a padded envelope.*
4. *They need hair from men and women, young and old, all colors and races.*

5. *Hair may be colored or permed, but not bleached or chemically damaged (if unsure, ask your stylist).*
6. *Hair swept off the floor is not usable.*
7. *Hair cut years ago is usable if it has been stored in a ponytail or braid.*
8. *Hair that is short, gray, or unsuitable for children will be separated from the ponytails and sold at fair market value to offset the cost of manufacturing.*
9. *You may pull curly hair straight to measure the minimum 10 inches.*
10. *The majority of all hair donated comes from children who wish to help other children.*
11. *Layered hair may be divided into multiple ponytails for donation.*

Christmas for Opal and Sean

If you want happiness, provide it to others.

Frank Tyger

"Okay, everyone, you can take your Christmas ornaments home today," Mr. Anthony said and passed around the ceramic figures we had made in art class. He handed a snowman to Jeremy and gave me the angel I made. I noticed Opal didn't get anything.

I asked, "Where's your ornament, Opal?"

Opal shrugged her shoulders. "I didn't make one. Who cares about a stupid ornament, anyway? We're not even getting a tree this year." She lowered her head so that her blonde hair covered her face. "My mom's cancer is back."

I didn't really know what cancer was, but I knew it was way worse than having the flu or chicken pox. The bell rang, and Opal ran out of class before I had a chance to say anything else.

All the way home, I thought of Opal and her little brother. Sean was always hanging around the store where my mom worked. At the end of the day, Mom would let him have all the donuts that didn't get sold. One time when I was in a bad mood, I said to Mom, "Why don't you bring those donuts home to me? I never get anything!"

"Yes, you do, Tiffany," Mom said. "You have more than you need of everything, and those donuts make Sean very happy. Why not let him have them?" I knew she was right. Once I saw Sean running home with a paper sack bulging with day-old donuts. He was grinning like he had a bag full of money instead of maple bars.

When I got home, I noticed something different about my house. My nose twitched as I tried to figure out what that good smell was. It reminded me of the time we went camping, and I collected pine cones. The sticky sap from the pine cones made my hands smell the same way. I ran to the living room and there it was—the biggest Christmas tree we'd ever had.

Mom said, "Surprise!" She was in the middle of the room, surrounded by boxes. Each box had CHRIST-MAS STUFF written on the side.

"I thought we weren't getting our tree until next weekend," I said.

"That's why it's a surprise, silly." Mom opened a box. Inside were red glass balls, sparkling like jewels. Plastic gingerbread people peeked out from under a pile of silver tinsel and glittering garland. Strands of gold beads spilled over the side of the box, like neck-laces in a pirate's treasure chest.

Mom put the lights on the tree, but she left the rest of the decorating up to me. I rummaged through the boxes, chewing on my bottom lip like I always do when I can't make up my mind. Should I use the sil-ver garland or the gold beads? The star I made in kindergarten, the puppy wearing a Santa Claus hat—every ornament was a favorite. Then there was my angel; I had to find a spot on the tree for her, too.

When I finished, every branch was loaded with dec-orations, and there was still a whole box of ornaments left.

Mom said, "Wow, is there a Christmas tree under all that? We have enough ornaments left over to deco-rate a second tree!"

That's when I remembered Opal and Sean. I was so excited about decorating our tree that I had almost forgotten about my friends missing out on Christmas. "Mom, we have to get another Christmas tree right away!" I shouted so loud that she almost dropped her glass of eggnog.

"Why? What's wrong with the one we have?" Mom looked confused.

"No, it's not for us. It's for Opal and Sean." I explained about Opal and Sean's mom being too sick for Christmas. It seemed like Mom didn't think my idea was so great because she was quiet for a long time. Then she said, "Well, get your coat. The tree lot closes in half an hour."

I rang the bell at Opal and Sean's house. Sean opened the door, nibbling on an apple fritter. He looked at the box marked CHRISTMAS STUFF in my arms, and then at the tree leaning against the porch rail. Sean's eyes got as round as ping-pong balls, and his eyebrows crawled up high on his forehead. Opal came to the door and said, "Tiffany! What are you doing here?"

"Hi, Opal," I said. "We didn't have room on our tree for all of these ornaments, and I know you didn't get a tree yet, so . . . "

"Way cool!" Sean said, jumping up and down. Opal smiled really big and helped Mom carry the tree inside. I was hardly through the door before Sean started opening the box. "Hey, Opal, look at this!" he said, digging through the decorations. "Here's a choo-choo train! And it lights up!"

A weak voice called from the other room. "Who's here, Opal?"

"Mom, it's Tiffany and her mother. They brought a Christmas tree," Opal shouted. My mom went to talk to Opal and Sean's mom.

"Thank you, Tiffany," Opal said.

"You're welcome," I said. "Oh, and here's one more ornament for your tree." I gave Opal the angel I made in class, and she hung it on the side of the tree that faced the window.

When Mom came back, her eyes were shining, like they did when she watched a sad movie on TV.

"We'd better go," Mom said. "Merry Christmas, kids."

As we walked home, I said, "We made Opal and Sean happy, didn't we, Mom?"

"Very happy," Mom agreed.

The fog was swirling around us, frizzing my hair and chilling my cheeks. Fog has a way of covering up all sounds, and I was glad to be walking with my mother in the silent night. Suddenly, I thought of something, and I just had to say it out loud. "Hey, Mom, I think I know why you give the donuts to Sean."

"Why?" Mom asked.

"Because when you make someone happy, it makes you feel happy, too!"

Tiffany O'Neill

8

LOOKING ON THE BRIGHT SIDE

I thought I'd never tie my shoe,
Until I did, and now I do.
I thought I'd never ride my bike,
And now I ride whenever I like.
I thought I'd never talk to you,
Now you're my friend, see what I can do?
I thought I'd never touch the sky,
But I never will unless I try.

Fonda Bell Miller

The Best Toys Ever

Imagination will often carry us to worlds that never were. But without it we go nowhere.

Carl Sagan

"It's not fair," I told my mother. "Every eight-year-old kid in the world has a GameCube."

"Not quite," she said.

"Yeah, I know. We don't."

Mom turned and gave me that "Are you being rude?" look, and I decided to back off. My mom was afraid I would turn into a couch potato with weak muscles and mush for a brain.

"Think of the eye-hand coordination I would gain from those games," I said hopefully. "The experience would probably double my test scores in school."

"So would reading a book," Mom said. She shook

her head and continued, "Why don't you go play in the sandpile or call a friend?"

The sandpile is Mom's answer to everything. Anytime we move somewhere new, the first two things she does is to get a library card and have Dad make a sandpile for us. I gotta admit, we have a neat sandpile—not one of those dorky plastic turtles filled with a bucket of sand. It took thirty bags of sand to make our sandpile. We have scraps of wood and old pipes and stuff for building. But still . . .

"Mommmmmm," I sighed. "No one wants to play at a house where there's no GameCube or video games. We don't even get cable, our TV screen is about six inches wide, and we don't have a DVD player. I can't invite kids over here. It's boring."

Mom frowned, and I knew I was getting to her. She wanted me to have friends. Maybe not every kid in the world had a GameCube, but everyone *I* knew did, and most of them had big-screen TVs with everything from HBO to Disney. Up until the year I was six, all I was allowed to watch was educational TV on our six-inch screen. Out in the sandpile, all the other kids would be playing some kind of superhero games. I was building stuff like on the home-building show. I was not going to be a couch potato, but I sure wasn't on my way to being popular.

I was not happy a few days later when Mom told me we were having people over for dinner. "They have a boy your age and a girl who is six," she said. "I want you to be polite and entertain them. This is a good chance to make a new friend with someone your own age."

It was just as I had expected. "So, what games do you have?" Brian asked. Somehow I knew he didn't mean checkers or chess or Chutes and Ladders.

Then his sister had to add, "We've just got Super Smash Brothers, and I unlocked just about all the characters."

I croaked out something about my GameCube being broken and maybe getting a new one. It was getting dark and too late for the sandpile, which I didn't think this kid was going to want to play in anyway. We sat around in my bedroom, tossed a Nerf ball, and poked at my box of Legos.

"So, where's the playroom?" the sister asked, snooping around out in the hallway.

"There's just the basement," I told her. "Only it's not fixed up."

"Let's see," she said as she started down to the first floor.

"I'll show you the way." I was hoping my mom would get the hint about how boring things were at our house.

Brian came, too.

It was dark and damp in the basement with a big old furnace to the right and a small bathroom with a sink and toilet. There were two light bulbs, one at each end of the huge room. We kept the bikes and sports equipment down there. You could see where the last family had started to fix it up with paint on one wall and tiles for the floor.

"What's all this?" Brian pointed at a pile of boxes and empty containers lined up along one of the walls.

"My mom saves all this stuff," I told him.

"What for?" the sister asked.

I shrugged my shoulders. How could I explain my mother's love of cardboard boxes, empty milk jugs, egg cartons, and green plastic tomato baskets? It all had to do with being creative and not catching the coach-potato disease.

Brian picked up a milk carton and tossed it in the air. He looked into a refrigerator box. "There must be a zillion milk cartons in there."

"Let me see." The sister tipped over the box with a crash, and Brian let out a whoop.

"We could build a fort," the sister suggested. But by the time we had emptied out the cartons, Brian had a better idea. We spent the next hour and a half flipping each other over in the box. We'd put the box down on its side. One of us would crawl in, lie flat, and yell, "Ready!" The other two kids would push the box over. *Whomp!* It made a great noise. But the waiting, just before the fall, was the best. Then we stuck our feet into bent plastic milk jugs and hopped across the floor without touching the cement.

Before I knew it, Brian's dad was calling down to us. "Let's go, kids. It's late." Brian's sister crawled into the box for one last fall.

"Ahhh, Dad . . . do we have to?" Brian asked.

"Yes! I want you two up here this minute."

Brian rolled his eyes and shrugged. I followed my

two guests up the stairs.

At the front door, the adults were getting coats out of the closet, saying thank you and good-bye, and making plans to get together again.

"Mom," Brian said, "they have the best toys ever. Can we come again?"

My mom looked at me suspiciously. Then she told Brian, "Sure, you can come again. Any time."

After they were gone, she stared at me. "Best toys ever?" She headed for the basement. I followed, sure I was about to get yelled at for getting into her things. I was going to have to clean up all by myself.

At the bottom of the stairs, Mom just stood still. "Best toys ever." She shook her head and smiled. The floor was covered with egg cartons and milk jugs. The battered refrigerator box was torn and beat up.

"I guess your friends weren't bored," Mom said. She didn't even ask me to clean up.

"No way," I said. I smiled and thought about some kids I might invite over after school on Monday.

Karen Lynn Williams

NO RODEO®

Reprinted by permission of Robert Berardi. ©2007 Robert Berardi.

The Best Present

The excellence of a gift lies in its appropriateness rather than in its value.

Charles Dudley Warner

"Katie Kingston is having a birthday party," I told my family. "And I'm invited!"

"Can I go, too?" my younger sister, Lynn, asked.

"Yes! Katie told me that both my sisters are invited. The party is at her house next Tuesday at one o'clock."

"That'll be fun for all of you," my mother said.

"Oh, I know it will be!" I replied. "Katie has so many things to play with—Barbie dolls and board games, dress-up clothes and jewelry. I remember going over to her house last Christmas. When I saw all her pres-ents, I was sure that Santa Claus thought more than one kid lived there."

"Maybe he got Katie's house mixed up with ours," my other sister, Sidney, said.

Lynn frowned. "What can we give Katie for her birthday? She already has everything."

"It sounds like she doesn't need any more toys," my mother said. She looked at the knickknack shelf over the couch and reached for a ceramic statue of a little girl.

"You can wrap this statue for her," she said, holding it out for us to see.

"No!" I cried. "I don't want to give Katie that old statue!"

The statue had been sitting on the living-room shelf for years. The blonde-haired girl was wearing a red dress, and she was bent forward, her hands behind her back. Her eyes were closed, and her lips were puckered into a kiss. A little boy statue had once stood next to her. His lips had been puckered into a kiss, too. But one day the statue of the little boy fell and broke into pieces.

"I want to get Katie a real present!" I said. "Something new!"

"It will be new to her," my mother said. "I'm sorry, but we can't afford to buy her anything at the store."

My excitement about the party disappeared. It would be embarrassing to give Katie the statue of the little girl. But I wanted to go to the party so much that I agreed.

My mother put the statue in a shoe box with tissue paper. If that wasn't bad enough, she wanted me to wrap the box in the wrapping paper from Sidney's last birthday. My mother always saved wrapping paper after birthdays and Christmas. She'd carefully peel off the tape and smooth out the paper. She saved ribbons and bows, too, if they were in good shape.

Grumbling, I taped a used pink bow on Katie's present.

"No one will know the difference," my mother said.

We didn't even buy a card. My sisters and I each folded a sheet of construction paper and drew a picture on the front with crayons. I drew a rose, Lynn drew a clown, and Sidney drew a doll. Inside we printed "Happy Seventh Birthday!" in our best handwriting.

On Tuesday afternoon, we walked across our country road under the hot summer sun and climbed the front steps of Katie's brick house. Sidney rang the doorbell, and Katie's mother led us into the quiet living room. Twisted crepe paper and pink balloons hung from the ceiling. Katie showed us the Barbie house she got from her parents that morning. The present in my hand felt lousy in comparison. I worried that it wasn't enough.

There were just the four of us. We played musical chairs, with Katie's mother turning the music on and off in the kitchen. I was the fastest to sit down and the last one left. Sidney pinned her tail on the donkey without even lifting her blindfold.

Afterward, we sat around a big table with pink paper plates and napkins. At each place was a small cup of candies and a tiny parasol that opened and closed. We put on hats and blew noisemakers that uncurled and squealed. It was so much fun.

Next, Lynn, Sidney, and I sang "Happy Birthday," and Katie blew out her candles. The cake was chocolate, and so was the icing.

Katie read each of the handmade cards. Then she looked over at our present with the pink bow. "Can I open my gift now?" she begged while her mother scooped vanilla ice cream onto our plates.

Her mother nodded, and my heart stood still. Katie picked up our present. She ripped the paper off the shoe box. "Shoes?" she asked.

"No," I said, feeling my heart thump. "Look inside."

Katie dug through the tissue paper and brought out the statue of the little girl. She had a puzzled look on her face, as if she was expecting a toy. I didn't feel like eating my cake anymore.

"Oh, isn't that sweet, Katie?" her mother said. "A little figurine. I think you're old enough now to have something breakable. You can put it on the shelf in your bedroom."

Katie smiled at us. "Thank you," she said.

"You're welcome," we answered and smiled back.

My mother had been right. The statue was new to Katie.

As my sisters and I said good-bye, Katie asked, "When can you come again?" She looked so lonely standing in the doorway and waving. I thought of how quiet it would be at her house after we were gone.

I knew then why she asked me over on Christmas, and why she invited my sisters and me to her birthday party. Katie didn't have everything after all. She had a lot of toys, but she had no one to play with. The statue was nice, but our best present to Katie that day was our friendship. We helped celebrate her birthday and make it special. Her mother couldn't have bought that in a store for all the money in the world.

Mary Laufer

Throwing Stones

Being deeply loved by someone gives you strength, while loving someone deeply gives you courage.

Lao Tzu

When I was eight, my dad built us the perfect house. Not just a house—a home on a cliff top overlooking the ocean. It was a happily-ever-after kind of home. But life isn't always a fairy tale.

I remember arriving home from school one day with my mom and little brother, our excited chatter spilling out of the car and filling the empty house. We were laughing at a joke my brother had told—he always got the punch line wrong—when we found Dad's cheery note:

Have just gone for a short run. Will be home soon.
Love, Dad

But he didn't come home. Eventually, Mom set out looking for him, and my brother and I went next door to my best friend's house to wait for her. The news, when it came, sprang at us from out of the blue. My friend's mom hung up the phone and had one of those concerned-adult looks on her face.

"Your dad has been taken to the hospital," she said, holding my brother and me tightly.

I could feel the rough lace of her shirt rubbing roughly against my cheek. I was confused by her concern because I thought hospitals were places where people went to get better. Kids at school returned with colorful casts on their arms, and we would sign them. They would come to school with crutches that we would borrow in the playground.

That afternoon, my friend and I jumped on the trampoline, sailing high in the air, and delighting at the way the warm breeze lifted our hair and tickled our cheeks. We talked about what we thought had happened to my dad, and when he might come home. We laughed about the future and planned what we would be when we grew up.

Unfortunately, my dad never left the hospital. He died that afternoon. Mom came home late that night, and before she could even say a word, I read the news in her eyes. Time slowed, and the world stopped spinning. My world went dark and silent.

That night, I lay in bed beside my mom, listening to her breathe into the dark. My whisper cut through the silence: "I can't believe he's gone."

"Neither can I." She sounded miles away, even though I could feel her warmth next to me. There was a long silence. Neither of us cried because that night we had no more tears to give.

"What do we do now?" I asked.

I still can't believe she had the strength and courage to answer such a big question. "Well, I guess we just keep trying to move forward. Together."

I wasn't sure if I could do that.

I had always loved the beach, but that year it became something sad for me. I had spent many days strolling along the salty shores with my dad, chasing seagulls and collecting shells. We had always shared our love of the beach—so how could I continue to love it without him?

Although I could no longer bear to walk along the sand, I often found myself down at the beach all the same. Instead of taking long walks in the tide, I began scrambling across the rocks at the top of the beach, often stumbling and hurting myself, but not really caring. One particularly difficult day, I picked up a small stone, threw it against a large rock, and watched it splinter into a million pieces. I could relate to that stone—I, too, felt broken and shattered. Again and again, I returned to the beach to throw stones, hurling all of my grief and sorrow and hurt against those rocks. They took all of my pain, but gave nothing back.

Having always been close to my mom, I turned to her one bleak day, telling her something that had been bothering me for a while.

"I never got to say good-bye to him."

She looked at me with her beautiful, searching eyes—eyes that knew me in a way no one else ever would. "Have you tried speaking to him?" she asked. *Speak to him?* For so long he had felt lost to me. Gone. Unreachable. How was I to find him?

One windy morning, while I watched my anger break against the rocks, one of my stones missed its target and sailed through the air to land with a soft patter on the salty sand. It lay not far from where Dad and I used to fish, pretending to be castaways catching our supper. I watched the ocean wash over the stone. When the waves receded, it was gone, as if my thoughts had been heard.

After that day, I started writing down my feelings on those stones and throwing them out into the ocean. They were like little messages to Dad, and for the first time since he had gone, I felt reconnected to him in some way. At first, the messages were sad and often angry. "How could you leave me?" I accused him. But, slowly, they changed. I told him that I still loved him and missed him, but that I knew he was watching over us. In time, I learned again to tell all my hopes and dreams to him.

In this way, I was able to keep moving forward as my mom always knew I had the strength to do. I never stopped throwing stones, but I learned to throw them out into the blue, toward the future. The beach came to mean something more to me after that—still sad, but hopeful. Knowing my dad was watching over us, I learned to enjoy the beach again, and often wandered hand-in-hand with my mom along the shore, watching my brother trail tiny footprints along the soft, pale sand ahead of us. Together.

Katherine Battersby

Wishing on a Lucky Star

My dog Lucy had a funny-shaped head. It was kind of sunken in above her ears. We found her like that. And even though she looked different, I thought she was the cutest dog I'd ever seen. Someone had given her up when they saw she was sick. So, we rescued Lucy and have taken care of her ever since.

I don't think Lucy knew she looked different than the other retrievers. She ran around the park just like every other dog and was always happy.

"C'mon, Lucy, you can do it," I remember saying when she first went in the pool. She was sniffing the water and put one paw in to test it out. I dribbled water onto her head, and she shook it off.

"I won't let you drown. C'mon, girl," I assured her. She trusted me and slowly climbed onto the first step, then the second. I clapped my hands. "I've got you, Loos. Come to me." She leapt into the pool and swam across like a pro. She even got the ball when I threw it in the pool. But the best was when she got out of the pool and shook off the water onto everyone sitting outside. She got everyone wet. It was so funny!

When Lucy turned five years old (which is thirty-five in people years), her legs started to shake. And then one day her tummy started getting fat, and she couldn't get up very well. My dad had to lift her up and carry her places. It looked like a hard job. Luckily, Dad was strong.

"We have to take Lucy to the hospital. She is very sick," Dad told us. It didn't sound good, and I was really scared. My brother, Eric, was only four, a few years younger than me. I don't think he understood how serious this was.

Mom, Dad, Eric, and I dropped Lucy off at the pet hospital and gave her a big hug. "I love you, Lucy," I said.

When we got home, I went into Eric's room. "We have to put all of our wishes together for Lucy to get better. Come into my room when it gets dark, and we'll start."

"Start what?" he asked.

"You'll see. Just come."

That night we waited for the stars to come out and wished on a star. "Now close your eyes," I said. "We wish that Lucy will come home from the doctor with a normal head, strong legs, and no more diseases. We wish that she'll get all better, so she can run around the park with all the other dogs again."

"Good one!" Eric said and smiled.

"We have to stick to this wish so it will be more powerful and come true."

"Okay, I promise," he agreed.

The next day, we wished on my eyelash. I blew it off my fingertip, and it flew away. That was a good sign. A couple days later, we went through a tunnel, and we made our wish again. I got it all in before we got out of the tunnel.

Eric and I took all the pennies out of my piggy bank before my soccer game. When we got to the park, I threw the pennies into the fountain one by one and made the same wish over and over again. Eric threw all of his in at the same time. I also snuck in a quarter because I thought it would be twenty-five times stronger since a quarter is worth twenty-five pennies.

The next night, we took a piece of cake out of the refrigerator and put a candle on it. We pretended it was Eric's birthday, and he made the wish and blew out the candle. We figured it was worth a try even though that wish might not count because it wasn't really his birthday.

Dad said he talked to the veterinarian, and Lucy was still very sick. The doctors didn't know if they could make her better, but wanted us to come to the pet hospital and visit her anyway.

When we got there, the doctor came out in his long white coat. He knelt down to Eric and me and told us that Lucy was too sick to live anymore. He said, "I heard you made lots of wishes, and I want you to know that because of all your good thoughts, a miracle happened. Lucy was pregnant when you brought her here, but too sick to have healthy puppies. But by some miracle, one survived. This little guy is so lucky because not only is he alive, but he is completely healthy, too."

Then he brought out the little puppy for us to see. He was so cute and looked like a little Lucy, with strong little legs, but no sunken-in head or diseases. But we couldn't take him home yet, not for a few weeks.

"What should we name him?" asked Mom.

"How about Lucky?" I suggested.

"I want Lucky! I want Lucky!" Eric chanted.

Mom and Dad loved the name and said it was just right for our new little pup.

Before we went to sleep, Eric and I looked out the window and up at the stars. "Thank you for giving us Lucy, who gave us Lucky. We'll take good care of him."

Who says wishes can't come true?

Melanie Joy Pastor

A Move to a New Life

I was stunned when my parents told me we were moving from Baton Rouge, Louisiana, to New York. First, I whined about not being able to make new friends and not knowing anything about New York.

My mom said, "You'll make new friends, and it's not like you know anything about Baton Rouge anyway."

I whined, "But I don't want to leave Louisiana. The weather is perfect here, and I love Cajun food!"

My mom glared at me and said, "You'll get used to the weather in New York, and you hate spicy food."

"But . . . but . . . but I don't want to go! I want to stay here."

"Well, we're going, so you might as well get packed. We're leaving on Monday." And she gave me a look that meant the conversation is over.

"Fine," I mumbled as I walked away.

I remember thinking about running away and joining a circus somewhere, but then I remembered that circus animals smell really bad, and I would miss my parents. So I shuffled around the house picking up random things, like my baseball and glove, and throwing them into a cardboard box. I felt like a big, heavy rain cloud was hanging over my head.

Within three days, all the furniture we were taking with us was packed into a moving van. Older things were on the lawn, ready to be sold at nowhere near what we paid for them. Little by little, our yard sale shrunk until no one even glanced at the gnawed coffee table, chewed-up plastic toys, and chipped coffee cups—all of which I had my teeth on at one time or another.

The next day was Monday, and we got up early to beat the traffic. I'll spare you the details of how boring it is to sit in a van and watch each tree as it whizzes by only to see another tree getting closer until it also passes by. Halfway there, we stopped at a motel to spend the night. This time, no one could sleep because of the smell coming from the heater in the room. By the time we made it to New York, it was the middle of the night, and my head was already drooping onto my shoulder.

When I woke up, I was expecting to find a smog-filled city where nothing grew. What I found was a city with plenty of grass, a school only two blocks from my new house, a supermarket within walking distance, and a neighborhood full of children my age who were willing to play with me and be my friends.

As I got used to this new setting, I realized that I didn't have to be afraid of changing where I lived and losing my friends. I could always make new friends, and the memories of my old friends would always be with me. I learned that change isn't scary, and that I should always look to the bright side of things and make the best of what I have. Now, when I face something new and intimidating, I don't think about all the bad things that can happen. I think of all the good things that will happen.

Andrew Sang

"Things are looking up."

Grandma's Wisdom

Letters are among the most significant memorial a person can leave behind them.

Johann Wolfgang von Goethe

The most valuable thing I own is a file that contains about fifty letters. The letters are from an old lady of eighty-four years—my grandmother. They may not have value in the eyes of a grown-up, but for a ten-year-old like myself, they are priceless pearls of wisdom passed on to a grandson by a grandmother who lived her life to the fullest.

My mom is an attorney, who spent most of her time working while I was growing up. My grandma looked after me and was like a second mother to me. Grandma was not very educated, but she had common sense. She showed me that life's simple pleasures bring us the most happiness, and that you cannot buy it with money.

Grandma used to take me for walks to show me the beauty in nature. While my parents spoiled me with expensive toys, I preferred her homemade toys, which she created with her own weary hands.

From the age of two, I can remember her reading to me. She introduced me to world-famous classics. By the time I was four, I was able to read classics like *Oliver Twist* and *Great Expectations.*

But when I was five, Grandma moved away to Australia. She was sad to leave, but after Granddad died, she found it difficult to manage on her own. My uncle, who lives in Australia, offered to help her out, so she agreed to go. She was sad, and I felt the same. I missed her right away. But then, one week after she left, a letter arrived.

> *Dear Grandson,*
> *I miss you a lot. But do you know absence makes hearts grow fonder? Write to me if you feel low and bored.*

So I started writing to her. I poured out all my problems into my letters. I was bullied in school, and I was called a brat by a kid who was older than me. I hated going to school after that.

I wrote to her:

> *Grandma,*
> *I'm being bullied at school. I feel hurt.*

She wrote back:

> *Dear Grandson,*

Just follow my instructions when the bully says something to hurt you. Tell him that you are hard of hearing and to repeat what he said again. He will repeat it. Keep on telling him that you did not hear, and he will get fed up and leave you alone.

I followed her instructions, and that was the end of the bullying.

Last year, we were having our annual sports meet at school. I've always hated sports. I would always come in last in races. All my classmates were stronger and older than me, and I couldn't compete with them. But my mom was forcing me to run in the race.

I wrote to Grandma:

Grandma, I'm not good in sports, but Mom is making me run in the race at school. I do not want to.

She wrote back:

Dear Grandson,
   I heard a song recently that had a wonderful message. There may be mountain peaks you have to climb on, there may be rivers fast and wide you may have to ride on. Unless you dream, unless you try, how will you know how far you can fly? Remember these words and believe in yourself.

So I participated in the event, and my classmate and I had to pass the ball between us four times and run to the finishing line. We managed to pass the ball without dropping it, and we made it to the line. The referee announced that we had won third prize out of seventeen children who were much stronger than us.

Once I returned home, I wrote to Grandma:

> *Thank you for your advice. I believed in myself and won*
> *third place in the race. I love you.*

Two weeks later, a package came in the mail. Grandma had sent a baseball cap and a pair of roller skates.

Letters passed between us every week. She often sent quotes by great people from newspapers and magazines. All of them, in one way or another, told me the same thing: "Believe in yourself, then you can reach even the farthest star."

I kept all of Grandma's letters in a file. When I felt low and sad, I would read them one by one. They lifted my spirits, and I came back to my old self again. Last week, a letter arrived.

> *Dear Grandson,*
> *I have bought a computer. I will be corresponding*
> *with you by e-mail.*

I checked my e-mail. Her letter had arrived. All the words were typed without using the space bar in between.

I wrote back:

> *Grandma, please use the space bar.*

She sent another e-mail.

> *Dear Grandson,*
> *I'm taking a computer course. I should improve on*

my typing by the time I finish in April.

I was shocked to hear that at eighty-four years of age, my grandma was taking a computer course. At ten, I felt tired after doing a little bit of homework! She taught me another lesson this time. There is no age limit to reach for the stars; you can reach them at ten . . . or eighty-four, if you only try a little harder each time.

The lessons my grandma taught in her letters will forever remain the most valuable and treasured possession I own.

Rahul de Livera, 10

Friends Are Like Flowers

I always think the flowers can see us and know what we are thinking about.

George Eliot

"He is so weird!" These words echoed in Daniel's ears every school day. He was the new kid in our small sixth-grade class. I watched Daniel lower his eyes as the so-called "cool" guys shoved him. Over the years, it had become my job to welcome the new kids to our school, but I figured it best to stay away from this one. He was just so . . . different. *What if the kids made fun of me, too?* Not that I was very popular or normal. I was the chubby girl with glasses, I couldn't play sports, I enjoyed musicals instead of rap and hip-hop, and I only had a few close friends. But I wasn't tortured like Daniel.

One night, my mom and I were having dinner. We talked and laughed until I brought up the subject of Daniel. I told her how oddly he acted, and that I wasn't sure I should be a friend to him because the other kids would laugh. My mom did something that affects me still today. She took me outside to the deck and said, "Michelle, look down at those flowers." The garden was beautiful. My parents had been working on it for years, and my mother was very proud of what her hands had made.

"Would you like the garden as much if there was only one kind of flower?"

"Of course not," I answered.

"Would you like all people to be the same then?" she asked.

"No . . ." I said. "I want them to be like flowers—different."

My mom smiled, and we silently walked back inside the house.

"Hi, Daniel. My name is Michelle!" I said the next day upon seeing him sitting alone at recess. We talked about school, music, TV, and flowers. It turns out we both grew orchids.

"I love orchids so much!" he said. "I love how there are so many different kinds, too!"

From that day forward until we graduated, Daniel was my best friend. We still keep in touch, and we still love orchids.

I am a freshman in high school now, and I am glad to be different. I'm not afraid to befriend someone who others think is odd. And I will always remember that friends should be like flowers—all different and all beautiful in their own way.

Michelle Marie

Who Is Jack Canfield?

Jack Canfield is the cocreator and editor of the Chicken Soup for the Soul series, which *Time* magazine has called "the publishing phenomenon of the decade." The series includes more than 140 titles with over 100 million copies in print in forty-seven languages. Jack is also the coauthor of eight other bestselling books, including *The Success Principles™: How to Get from Where You Are to Where You Want to Be, Dare to Win, The Aladdin Factor, You've Got to Read This Book,* and *The Power of Focus: How to Hit Your Business, Personal and Financial Targets with Absolute Certainty.*

Jack has recently developed a telephone coaching program and an online coaching program based on his most recent book, *The Success Principles.* He also offers a seven-day Breakthrough to Success seminar every summer, which attracts 400 people from about fifteen countries around the world.

Jack is the CEO of Chicken Soup for the Soul Enterprises and the Canfield Training Group in Santa Barbara, California, and is founder of the Foundation for Self-Esteem in Culver City, California. He has conducted intensive personal and professional development seminars on the principles of success for more than a million people in twenty-nine countries around the world. Jack is a dynamic keynote speaker, and he has spoken to hundreds of thousands of others at more than 1,000 corporations, universities, professional conferences, and conventions and has been seen by millions more on national television shows such as *Oprah, Montel, The Today Show, Larry King Live, Fox and Friends, Inside Edition, Hard Copy, CNN's Talk Back Live, 20/20, Eye to Eye,* and the *NBC Nightly News* and the *CBS Evening News.* Jack was also a featured teacher in the hit movie *The Secret.*

Jack is the recipient of many awards and honors, including three honorary doctorates and a Guinness World Records Certificate for having seven books from the Chicken Soup for the Soul series appearing on the *New York Times* bestseller list on May 24, 1998.

To write to Jack or for inquiries about Jack as a speaker, his coaching programs, trainings, or seminars, use the following contact information:

Jack Canfield
The Canfield Companies
P.O. Box 30880 • Santa Barbara, CA 93130
phone: 805-563-2935 • fax: 805-563-2945
e-mail: info4jack@jackcanfield.com
website: www.jackcanfield.com

Who Is Mark Victor Hansen?

In the area of human potential, no one is more respected than Mark Victor Hansen. For more than thirty years, Mark has focused solely on helping people from all walks of life reshape their personal vision of what's possible. His powerful messages of possibility, opportunity, and action have created powerful change in thousands of organizations and millions of individuals worldwide.

He is a sought-after keynote speaker, bestselling author, and marketing maven. Mark's credentials include a lifetime of entrepreneurial success and an extensive academic background. He is a prolific writer with many bestselling books, such as *The One Minute Millionaire, The Power of Focus, The Aladdin Factor,* and *Dare to Win,* in addition to the Chicken Soup for the Soul series. Mark has had a profound influence through his library of audios, videos, and articles in the areas of big thinking, sales achievement, wealth building, publishing success, and personal and professional development.

Mark is the founder of the MEGA Seminar Series. MEGA Book Marketing University and Building Your MEGA Speaking Empire are annual conferences where Mark coaches and teaches new and aspiring authors, speakers, and experts on building lucrative publishing and speaking careers. Other MEGA events include MEGA Marketing Magic and My MEGA Life.

He has appeared on television (*Oprah,* CNN, and *The Today Show*), in print (*Time, U.S. News & World Report, USA Today, New York Times,* and *Entrepreneur*), and on countless radio interviews, assuring our planet's people that "You can easily create the life you deserve." As a philanthropist and humanitarian, Mark works tirelessly for organizations such as Habitat for Humanity, American Red Cross, March of Dimes, Childhelp USA, and many others. He is the recipient of numerous awards that honor his entrepreneurial spirit, philanthropic heart, and business acumen. He is a lifetime member of the Horatio Alger Association of Distinguished Americans, an organization that honored Mark with the prestigious Horatio Alger Award for his extraordinary life achievements.

Mark Victor Hansen is an enthusiastic crusader of what's possible and is driven to make the world a better place.

Mark Victor Hansen & Associates, Inc.
P.O. Box 7665
Newport Beach, CA 92658
phone: 949-764-2640 • fax: 949-722-6912
website: www.markvictorhansen.com

Who Is Patty Hansen?

Patty Hansen, with her partner, Irene Dunlap, authored *Chicken Soup for the Kid's Soul, Chicken Soup for the Kid's Soul 2, Chicken Soup for the Preteen Soul, Chicken Soup for the Preteen Soul 2, Chicken Soup Christmas Treasury for Kids,* and *Chicken Soup for the Girl's Soul*—all books that kids love to read and use as guides for everyday life. Patty is also a contributor to some of the most-loved stories in the Chicken Soup for the Soul series, coauthor of *Condensed Chicken Soup for the Soul* (Health Communications, Inc.), and *Out of the Blue: Delight Comes into Our Lives* (HarperCollins). Because of her love for preteens, Patty created www.preteenplanet.com, a website to give preteens a fun and safe cyberspace experience where they can also become empowered to make their world a better place. Check it out!

Prior to her career as an author, Patty worked for United Airlines as a flight attendant for thirteen years. During that time, she received two commendations for bravery. She received the first one when (as the only flight attendant on board) she prepared forty-four passengers for a successful planned emergency landing. The second was for single-handedly extinguishing a fire on board a mid-Pacific flight, which averted an emergency situation and saved hundreds of lives.

Patty is the president of legal and licensing for Chicken Soup for the Soul Enterprises, Inc., and has helped to create an entire line of Chicken Soup for the Soul products and licenses.

Patty shares her home life with her two daughters, Elisabeth, 21, and Melanie, 19; grandson, Seth, age two; her mother, Shirley; housekeeper and friend, Dora; two rabbits, four horses, three dogs, five cats, four birds, thirty-two fish, eight pigeons, thirty-six chickens (yes, they all have names), a haven for hummingbirds, and a butterfly farm.

If you would like to contact Patty:

Patty Hansen
P.O. Box 10879
Costa Mesa, CA 92627
e-mail: patty@preteenplanet.com
website: www.preteenplanet.com

Who Is Irene Dunlap?

Irene Dunlap, coauthor of *Chicken Soup for the Kid's Soul*, *Chicken Soup for the Kid's Soul 2*, *Chicken Soup for the Preteen Soul*, *Chicken Soup for the Soul Christmas Treasury for Kids*, *Chicken Soup for the Preteen Soul 2*, and *Chicken Soup for the Girl's Soul* began her writing career in elementary school when she discovered her love for creating poetry, a passion she believes to have inherited from her paternal grandmother. She went on to express her love for words through writing fictional short stories, lyrics, as a participant in speech competitions, and eventually as a vocalist.

During her college years, Irene traveled around the world as a student of the Semester at Sea program aboard a ship that served as a classroom, as well as home base, for over 500 college students. After earning a bachelor of arts degree in communications, she became the media director of Irvine Meadows Amphitheatre in Irvine, California, and eventually co-owned an advertising and public-relations agency that specialized in entertainment and health-care clients.

In February 2004, Irene released her first book in a series titled *TRUE—Real Stories About God Showing Up in the Lives of Teens*, in order to encourage teens and young adults in their faith. *TRUE Volume 2* followed in August 2007.

While creating difference-making books, Irene continues to carry on a singing career, performing various styles of music, but specializing in jazz.

Irene lives in Newport Beach, California, with her husband, Kent, daughter, Marleigh, son, Weston, and Australian shepherd, Gracie. In her spare time, Irene enjoys horseback riding, gardening, cooking, and painting. If you are wondering how she does it all, she will refer you to her favorite Bible passage for her answer—Ephesians 3:20.

If you would like to contact Irene, write to her at:

Irene Dunlap
P.O. Box 10879
Costa Mesa, CA 92627
e-mail: irene@lifewriters.com
website: www.LifeWriters.com

Contributors

Angela Abbott is a fifth-grade teacher known for her innovative teaching strategies and ability to inspire both teachers and students. She holds a master's degree in education from Pennsylvania State University, was named Wal-Mart Teacher of the Year, and speaks professionally for Abbott Learning (www.abbottlearning.org). Angela can be contacted at abbottlearning@yahoo.com.

Lara Anderson received her bachelor of arts, with honors, in English and writing from California State University, San Bernardino, in 1992. There she published and edited the *Pacific Review* journal and received the Sandra Fredrickson Award for poetry. She published a photography and poetry book, *An Echo for a Cliff*. She now teaches high school in Los Angeles and publishes short stories for elementary-school textbooks. She plans to publish children's stories, novels, and screenplays. Please contact her at purpletrees@sbcglobal.net.

Katherine Battersby is an occupational therapist who works as a counselor with children in Brisbane, Australia. She is returning to the university this year to study design, in order to further her goal to one day both write and illustrate books for young people. Please e-mail her at katherinebattersby@iinet.net.au.

Robert Berardi was born in 1968 in New York and educated at University of the Arts, Philadelphia. He writes and draws *No Rodeo*, a comic strip about a preteen girl named Desiree. *No Rodeo* can be seen on PreteenPlanet.com. Contact Robert at robtberardi@yahoo.com.

Jessica Bolandrina is a senior in high school (Class of 2007) and plays the piano and banduria. She participated in the Asian American Writer's Workshop's 2006 "Where I'm Calling From" program in New York City.

Kathleen Bracher is a born Hoosier and lives in Boonville, Indiana. She lived for fourteen years in Germany, helping in mission work. She enjoys reading, horseback riding, and writing short stories for people of all ages.

Robin Smith Bridges resides with her family in Amherst, New York. A police detective and Buffalo State College graduate, she passionately enjoys writing for children. "Friends of the Heart" is a story of Christian spirit as experienced by her daughter, Ariana. Robin is currently writing a picture book. Please e-mail her at rsbridges@adelphia.net.

Richard Brookton is a retired schoolteacher from Australia. He and his wife, Natalie, have two married children. As a boy, he lived in Silverwater, a suburb of Sydney. His teaching career started in one-teacher schools in the Australian bush, and he later taught high school and science college classes. Barbershop singing (lead and tenor) is now one of his passions.

Stephanie Ray Brown of Henderson, Kentucky, is proud to be Terry's wife, Savannah and Cameron's mom, Rita's daughter, and the ESS reading and writing teacher at Niagara Elementary School. She dedicates her story to her mother, who always made holidays special even though, as a single mother, she was on a shoestring budget. Stephanie challenges her Niagara students and staff, who are some of her biggest writing cheerleaders, to write their own Chicken Soup for the Soul stories. Remember, everyone has a story to be told, and *you* are the only person who can tell it! She can be reached at savvysdad@aol.com.

John P. Buentello is an elementary schoolteacher in San Antonio, Texas. He is the author of fiction and nonfiction for children. He also writes science fiction, fantasy, and mysteries. John is pursuing his Ph.D. in literature and is at work on his second novel. He can be reached at jakkhakk@yahoo.com.

Renie Burghardt, born in Hungary, is a freelance writer. She has been published in several Chicken Soup for the Soul books, *Guideposts* books, *Cup of Comfort, Rocking Chair Reader*, and others. She lives in the country and loves nature, animals, and spending time with her family and friends. Please e-mail her at renie_burghardt@yahoo.com.

Arlene Y. Burke received her B.S. and M.S. degrees in education in the sixties and seventies. She has taught elementary through high school. In 1987, she began a second career with IBM, and retired in December 2005. She plans to write inspirational children's books, adult fiction, and creative nonfiction.

Karen Cogan received her bachelor of arts degree in education from the University of Houston. She currently teaches kindergarten at a neighborhood school. She also enjoys writing inspirational stories and articles. She is a published author of adult fiction books and children's books. You can view her website at www.karencogan.com.

Amy Cornell is twelve years old, and her favorite sixth-grade classes are English and art. Amy enjoys writing stories, poetry, and lyrics, playing the piano, and producing home music videos. When Amy becomes an adult, she would like to pursue a career in teaching or photography.

Cookie Curci was born and raised in San Jose, California (Silicon Valley). This fruitful area of California was home to her immigrant grandparents, from whom she inherited a bounty of generational traditions, life lessons, and family anecdotes. Many of Cookie's stories reflect these family memories. She has also written several articles for the *San Francisco Chronicle*, as well as for senior newspapers, websites, and books.

Eleven-year-old **Emylee Cuthbertson** has shown a genuine compassion for animals since she was a toddler. Her special way with animals has gained responses that elude others. As a bird-watcher and nature lover, Emylee hones her appreciation for our environments for all living creatures. At her home, she enjoys the camaraderie of two dogs, a cat, and a small herd of comical pet chickens.

Rahul de Livera is twelve years old and a student in Australia. He is a Sri Lankan by birth, and migrated to Australia in 2006. He started writing at the age of six, and his stories were published in the *Shanker Children's Art Number*. He was very close to his grandma, who passed away four months after his arrival in Australia.

Mary Lou DeCaprio was previously published in *Chicken Soup for the Kid's Soul 2* and has recently published a picture book titled *The Lost Feather*. She enjoys substitute teaching, volunteering, and watching old movies with her husband and four children. She can be reached at www.thelostfeather.com.

Christopher Geren was born and raised in Las Vegas, Nevada. He was raised by two amazing parents and a stepfather and has recently moved to Los Angeles to develop a career in the creative arts.

Sandy Green lives with her husband and children in Virginia. Her work has been published in *Highlights for Children, Fandangle, Dragonfly Spirit,* and *KidVisions*. Andy was ten when he played for the Blues. Now, at thirteen, he's played with the All Stars and started this season with the Green team.

Dontay Hall is an eighth-grade student who enjoys reading the Bible and playing basketball and video games. He has been published in several kids' magazines, including *Nick Jr.* and *Kate Harper's Greeting Cards*. His nana, Evelyn Hall, has written a series of children's books about him. You can order one of her books at www.lulu.com.

Talia Haven lives in Michigan with her husband and is currently working on her first picture-book manuscript. This is her first story for the Chicken Soup for the Soul series.

Jonny Hawkins is a full-time freelance cartoonist from Sherwood, Michigan. Thousands of his cartoons appear in magazines, books, and online. His calendars, *Medical Cartoon-A-Day* and *Fishing Cartoon-A-Day* can be found online and in bookstores along with his books.

Renee Hixson survives on a small college campus where her husband is vice president. As a mom of teens and several Korean home-stay students, and as a night janitor, Renee observes much of life's dramas. Writing is her only defense against insanity. Please e-mail this hopelessly flawed but optimistic writer at rhixson@telus.net.

Carly Hurwitz is seventeen years old and a junior in high school. She enjoys writing short stories and film reviews in her spare time. She hopes to major in early childhood education.

Ann Ingalls is the mother of three grown children, a teacher, and professed "word nerd." She and her husband, Winston, love to travel far and wide, ride bikes, eat barbecue, listen to jazz, and spoil their cats, Harry and Lucy. When she grows up, she hopes to be a grandmother.

Kristie Jones currently works as the children's librarian at Cairns Libraries in Queensland, Australia. Since being shortlisted for the Queensland Young Writers Award, she has written and published a number of short stories particularly for children.

Kendal Kornacki loves her family and her dog. She enjoys running, working hard in school, and getting together with her friends.

Virginia L. Kroll has had forty-seven children's books published since 1992 and over 1,700 items in magazines. She is married and lives in Hamberg, New York, with her family, which includes three daughters, three sons, a granddaughter, and thirty-six pets.

Lana Krumwiede's stories and poems have appeared in many children's magazines, such as *Babybug, Spider, The Friend, Appleseeds,* and *Fun for Kidz*. She earned a master's degree from Washington State

University in 1999. The story of "Swimming on a Goat" happened to her sister-in-law, who grew up in Czechoslovakia. The story of "Making Friends with a Puppet" happened to her when she was in third grade.

Mary Laufer is a freelance writer who lives in Forest Grove, Oregon. She began writing in fourth grade and never gave up the dream of seeing her stories in print. Her other works appear in *Chicken Soup for the Girl's Soul, Cicada*, and *Her Story: What I Learned in My Bathtub*.

Machille Legoullon is the mother of four boys, who range in age from seven to twenty-three. Her passion is children's writing, and she currently writes for a local parenting magazine, *Community Kids*. She has written several picture-book manuscripts and is working on her first novel for young adults.

Annie Loveless was eleven when she wrote the poem "My Hope for the World." Now, she is sixteen years old and a junior in high school. Annie takes honors classes and plans to go to college to study forensics. She enjoys riding dirt bikes and singing.

Dania Denise Mallette, twenty-three, is a San Francisco State University graduate with a major in broadcast journalism and a minor in journalism. Dania enjoys drawing, reading, and writing. She is currently working on getting her first television news-reporting job, but plans to continue her writing projects. Please e-mail her at DaniaMallette@gmail.com.

Bryan Martinez, age fifteen, enjoys hanging out with friends and family from church. Bryan's favorite classes are physical education and French 2. He would like to become a lawyer. Bryan enjoyed writing his story and would like to write more in the future.

Mallory McGinty enjoys playing basketball and softball, taking dance lessons, and spending time with her friends. She lives with her mom, dad, little brother, guinea pig, and two special cats, Sox and Sierra, who were both adopted from the Humane Society.

Sarah McIver has a passion for written words and understands how powerful they can be. She has directed her efforts toward copywriting for the fundraising sector to encourage more donations toward worthy causes. Sarah is a loving wife and proud mother who lives in Gibraltar, Europe. Please contact her at hdazsgirl@hotmail.com.

Theresa (Terri) Meehan shares memories of her childhood in "Being True to Myself." The story takes place in Warren, Ohio, in 1965 when the author was eight years old. She resides in England with her husband. Theresa likes writing inspirational stories. Many have been published, including poetry for an upcoming Chicken Soup for the Soul book.

Jacqueline (Jacki) J. Michels is a mother of five, the wife of one, and a friend to many. She is a columnist and the author of several yet-to-be-published children's stories. Please contact her at jjoila@hotmail.com.

Fonda Bell Miller taught primary-age children for eighteen years. She is now a poet and writer living with her daughter and husband in Alexandria, Virginia. Please e-mail her at FMiller603@aol.com.

Esme Sky Mills has always hoped to find a secret treasure map hidden in an old diary, but has stopped looking in other people's diaries. She lives on Pender Island, British Columbia, with her two amazing boys. She is hard at work on a teen novel and can be reached at esmesky@cablelan.net.

Christine Mix is a children's illustrator. "Standing Up" is one of her childhood memories written in her adult years. She is currently forty-four years old. Her illustrations have appeared in *Write Out of the Oven*, by Josephine Waltz. For more information, visit Christine's website at www.chrismixart.com or contact her at cmixart@yahoo.com.

Felicia Moore was born in Riverside, California. She now resides in Detroit, Michigan. She is a housewife who has always enjoyed writing songs and poems. "Granny's Hands" was inspired by the death of her granny, Fannie Ruth Moore.

Tiffany O'Neill was raised in California's Central Valley and now makes her home in New Jersey, where she is a full-time wife and mother. She is currently working on her first novel for young adults. Please e-mail her at oneill_tiffany@yahoo.com.

Mark Parisi's "Off the Mark" comic panel has been syndicated since 1987 and is distributed by United Media. Mark's humor also graces greeting cards, T-shirts, calendars, magazines, newsletters, and books. Please visit his website at www.offthemark.com. Lynn, his wife and business partner, and their daughter, Jen, contribute with inspiration (as do three cats).

Melanie Pastor is a first-grade teacher in Encino, California. She has a B.A. in sociology and a master's in education. She wrote the story "Wishing on a Lucky Star" as a teenager for a school assignment about "something good that came out of something bad." Melanie just published her first picture book titled, *Wished for One More Day*. During the summer she teaches swimming lessons. She loves Rollerblading, swimming, skiing, and traveling. Please e-mail her at melanie pastor@msn.com.

Lloret Pelayo is currently a senior in high school, and plans to major in psychology and criminology. Lloret was born in Chicago, where her story takes place. She enjoys writing short stories and poems.

Sherm Perkins was a teacher, coordinator, and director in an at-risk school in Cincinnati, Ohio, before retiring in the spring of 2006 to devote more time to his wife, Connie, his two sons, Nate and Kevin, and his first love, writing. Please e-mail him at gratis74@msn.com.

Karissa Porter is fourteen years old and goes to middle school. She enjoys hanging out with her friends and playing outdoors. She started writing when she was six years old and is hopeful that she will continue writing for the rest of her life.

Jamuna Rangachari writes on varied subjects, with a focus on children's fiction and spirituality. Two of her books have been published, and she contributes regularly to various publications. She currently lives in Delhi, India, with her husband and two children. You may visit her at www.jamunarangachari.com or e-mail her at jamuna. rangachari@gmail.com.

Ronnie Ray Reese has been published in several magazines. His audience is religious, secular, children, juniors, teens, and adults. You can reach him at ronnierayreese@yahoo.com.

Nicole Rinaldi is thirteen years old and in the eighth grade. She loves music and her friends. Her hobbies are writing poems, swimming, and photography. Her favorite type of poem to write is about love. She loves riding her bike around her neighborhood. She's a busy girl.

Angela Rooker is currently a sophomore in high school. She likes to read. After high school she plans to become an anthropologist.

Michelle Rossi received her bachelor of science, with honors, in elementary education from Oakland University in Michigan. She teaches a curriculum she has designed herself called *All About Me* to many different communities. Michelle enjoys spending time with family and friends and writing. Please visit her websites at www.lulu.com/allaboutme and www.marrossproductions.com.

Joi Sampsell, a former preschool and art teacher from Ohio, now resides in Floral City, Florida. She enjoys painting, the art of book making, and writing children's stories. She earned a bachelor of arts degree from Eckerd College in St. Petersburg, Florida. She is the proud mother of four sons and six grandchildren, the inspirations for her stories.

Andrew Sang is a high school student and is on the boys gymnastics team. He tries as hard as he can and continues to get better at gymnastics and at life. He also enjoys drawing, dancing, and break dancing.

Becca Sherman is currently enrolled at Wake Forest University, and plans to study political science and economics. She loves basketball and volleyball, and is a waitress at the local Outback restaurant. Feel free to contact her via e-mail at sherre6@wfn.edu.

Christine M. Smith is the mother of three, grandmother of thirteen, and foster mother to many others. She has been married to her husband, James, for thirty-eight years, and loves reading and writing, church activities, and spending time with her family. Please e-mail her at iluvmyfamilyxxx000@yahoo.com.

Darian Smith is in the seventh grade and is a first-time author. Although she plans to continue writing, she also has a passion for art and basketball, and enjoys going to her church youth group. She loves her family and friends (including Jenna, who is still her best friend) and appreciates their support.

Joseph "Silly" Sottile, author of *Picture Poetry on Parade*, loves writing children's poems and stories. He's a frequent classroom visitor and writing instructor. His poetry website for kids (www.joe-sottile.com) provides inspiration and poetry "recipes," while featuring a monthly contest. Please e-mail him at jsottile@frontiernet.net.

Ruth B. Spiro lives in Illinois with her husband and two daughters, who provide endless inspiration for her writing. Her articles and essays have appeared in *Child, Woman's World,* and *Family Fun.* She is also the author of a children's book, *The Bubble Gum Artist*. She can be reached at www.ruthspiro.com.

Charlotte Uteg has written in her free time since kindergarten and also enjoys reading fiction. She likes drawing and Japanese culture, hanging out with her friends role playing, and soccer. She is the leader of a large group of friends and enjoys planning parties and holidays. She will graduate from high school this year and move on to college.

Sirena Van Schaik is an early childhood educator who graduated with honors from Mohawk College in 2001. She enjoys reading, writing, scrapbooking, and just spending time with her husband, two children, and two Labrador retrievers. Sirena is currently finishing her first novel and has plans for many more.

Karen Lynn Williams is in graduate writing programs at Chatham College and Seton Hill University. She has published ten books for children, including the award-winning *Galimoto*. She has four children and has lived in Maiwai and Haiti, where a number of her books are set. She enjoys traveling, cross country skiing, hiking, quilting, and writing. Please e-mail her at williams.writes@verizon.net.

Victoria D. Williams is a thirteen-year-old eighth-grader. Victoria loves reading, writing, and playing video games. Her great love of animals, especially her dog, Hunter, promotes her desire to one day become a veterinarian.

Permissions

We would like to acknowledge the many publishers and individuals who granted us permission to reprint the cited material.

Thinking of Others. Reprinted by permission of Jessica Dawn Bolandrina and Gretheline Bolandrina. ©2005 Jessica Dawn Bolandrina.

My Lady. Reprinted by permission of Sirena Van Schaik. ©2006 Sirena Van Schaik.

The Right Thing to Do. Reprinted by permission of Stephanie Ray Brown. ©2006 Stephanie Ray Brown.

Friends of the Heart. Reprinted by permission of Robin A. Bridges. ©2006 Robin A. Bridges.

The Key to Bethany's Heart. Reprinted by permission of Karen Cogan. ©2006 Karen Cogan.

Bossy Lara. Reprinted by permission of Lara Denise Anderson. ©2004 Lara Denise Anderson.

A Special Lunch. Reprinted by permission of Christopher Geren. ©2004 Christopher Geren.

The Twenty-Dollar Bill. Reprinted by permission of Mallory McGinty and Jennifer McGinty. ©2006 Mallory McGinty.

Sometimes, Babies Get in the Way. Reprinted by permission of Ruth B. Spiro. ©2006 Ruth B. Spiro.

Being a Team Player. Reprinted by permission of Annie Allena Loveless and Kathleen Loveless. ©2001 Annie Allena Loveless.

For the Love of Animals. Reprinted by permission of Emylee Percazy Ivy Cuthbertson and Linda Lee Purvis. ©2006 Emylee Percazy Ivy Cuthbertson.

Second Act. Reprinted by permission of John P. Buentello. ©2006 John P. Buentello.

Music Is Contagious. Reprinted by permission of Mary Lou DeCaprio. ©1992 Mary Lou DeCaprio.

Standing Up. Reprinted by permission of Christine Ann Mix. ©2006 Christine Ann Mix.

Someone to Count On. Reprinted by permission of Richard Tucker Brookton. ©2006 Richard Tucker Brookton.

The Gravel Pit. Reprinted by permission of Renee Willa Hixson. ©2006

Renee Willa Hixson.

Adam Gets to Play. Reprinted by permission of Talia Haven. ©2006 Talia Haven.

Swimming on a Goat. Reprinted by permission of Lana M. Krumwiede. ©2005 Lana M. Krumwiede.

The Gift Givers Club. Reprinted by permission of Kendal Kornacki and Claudia Kornacki. ©2000 Kendal Kornaki.

Being Responsible. Reprinted by permission of Nicole M. Rinaldi and Steve Rinaldi. ©2006 Nicole Rinaldi.

Who Let the Dogs Out? Reprinted by permission of Arlene Y. Avery Burke. ©2006 Arlene Y. Avery Burke.

My Very Own Dog. Reprinted by permission of Kathleen Elizabeth Bracher. ©2006 Kathleen Elizabeth Bracher.

Who's to Blame? Reprinted by permission of Michelle Rossi. ©2005 Michelle Rossi.

Following the Rules. Reprinted by permission of Joseph James Sottile. ©2006 Joseph James Sottile.

The Hill. Reprinted by permission of Sherman Eugene Perkins. ©2003 Sherman Eugene Perkins.

A Little Birdie . . . a Big Responsibility. Reprinted by permission of Dania Denise Mallette. ©2005 Dania Denise Mallette.

Munchy. Reprinted by permission of Lloret Demar Pelayo and Maribel D. Pelayo. ©2006 Lloret Demar Pelayo.

Making Good Choices. Reprinted by permission of Dontay Hall and Evelyn Hall. ©2005 Dontay Hall.

Starting Over. Reprinted by permission of Jamuna Rangachari. ©2006 Jamuna Rangachari.

Friends Forever. Reprinted by permission of Darian Smith and Jane Smith. ©2006 Darian Smith.

Max and the Purple BMX Mongoose Bike. Reprinted by permission of Joi Sampsell. ©2006 Joi Sampsell.

Being True to Myself. Reprinted by permission of Theresa Meehan. ©2005 Theresa Meehan.

Is Sixteen Enough? Reprinted by permission of Christine Mae Smith. ©2006 Christine Mae Smith.